A GIFT FOR: _____

FROM: _____

DATE: _____

ORGANIZING
FOR THE
Rest OF US

100 Realistic Strategies to Keep
Any House Under Control

Dana K. White

THOMAS NELSON
Since 1798

Organizing for the Rest of Us

© 2022 Dana K. White

Published in Nashville, Tennessee, by Thomas Nelson. Thomas Nelson is a registered trademark of HarperCollins Christian Publishing, Inc.

Published in association with literary agent Tawny Johnson of Illuminate Literary Agency, www.illuminateliterary.com.

Photographer: Lauren Brown

Thomas Nelson titles may be purchased in bulk for educational, business, fund-raising, or sales promotional use. For information, please email SpecialMarkets@ThomasNelson.com.

ISBN 978-1-4002-3143-0 (HC)
ISBN 978-1-4002-3142-3 (audiobook)
ISBN 978-1-4002-3144-7 (eBook)

Printed in China

22 23 24 25 26 WAI 10 9 8 7 6 5 4 3 2 1

CONTENTS

INTRODUCTION

Here's my promise to you for this book: everything you read here will be based in reality. Keeping a house under control is not natural for me. My home used to turn into a disaster zone again and again, no matter how many quick tips or nifty tricks I tried. I eventually hit rock bottom and started an anonymous blog where I recorded my thoughts and processes as I worked to figure out what I was doing wrong and what I should be doing instead.

I eventually figured it out. Tips help, but no "simple trick" will magically turn your house into the one you dream about. That's why we're calling these *strategies*. Some of them will be quick to implement and will make the overall process of changing your home easier, but others are mindset shifts and changes to the way you do day-to-day tasks that will ultimately make a bigger difference than storing your toothbrush in a different container.

As someone who audibly groaned at promises of quick fixes for my lifetime of messiness, I'm excited to share what I've learned in the bite-size, easy-to-grasp-and-implement format of this book. There's a lot of value in that. But if you need more words, more answers to all your what-ifs and but-what-abouts, I've got those too. They're in my other books, *Decluttering at the Speed of Life* and *How to Manage Your Home Without Losing Your Mind*. Feel free to continue your organizing and decluttering journey with those helpful resources!

- *Part 1* -

MINDSET
SHIFTS

UNDERSTAND THE LAYERS
OF A CLEAN HOUSE

Have you ever stared in awe at a friend's clean home and wondered, *What in the world do they do that I don't do?* Or have you felt like your head might explode when that friend claims she "never cleans"? Let me explain what People Like Them know that People Like Me don't: there are three layers of a clean house, and cleaning is the last layer. If the first two layers are peeled back, cleaning won't be as daunting.

The first layer that has to be removed to get to a clean house is clutter. It simply isn't possible to clean a surface, space, or room that is piled with stuff. Decluttering has to happen for a house to look clean, be cleaned, and stay clean. Quick cleaning tips don't make much of an impact in a house that's overloaded with stuff.

The second layer of a clean house is daily stuff. Certain tasks need to be done every single day, or at least almost

every day. (I will teach you the four daily tasks to start with.) Doing a week's worth of dishes isn't cleaning your house; it's catching up on daily stuff. Picking up toys or shoes or math worksheets from the living room floor isn't cleaning; it's picking up. Not doing the absolute basics every day means that when you "clean," you spend hours excavating the kitchen. By the time you're done, all the cleaning energy you started with is gone.

The third layer is the actual cleaning: dusting, vacuuming, mopping, wiping, and scrubbing. When my house was full of clutter, I was forever behind on daily tasks. "Cleaning my house" was a huge and daunting project that I continually put off.

Once I peeled back the first two layers of a clean house,

I understood those people with perfectly fine houses who said they "never cleaned." They were talking about actual cleaning. That's the beauty of understanding the layers of a clean house. If layers one and two are under control, layer three doesn't feel so urgent.

So, yes, this book will contain tips and tricks, but I want you to know that I understand those of you who balk at "Ten Easy Ways to Keep Your House Perfect" lists. I understand, because there was a time when I didn't understand—and that's the perspective from which I write this book.

UNDERSTAND WHAT CLUTTER IS AND FIND YOUR CLUTTER THRESHOLD

I define clutter as anything that continually gets out of control in my own home. Defining clutter this way has improved my home because this definition means clutter is no longer an ambiguous idea. I no longer need to evaluate each item in my home for its potential to be used in the future or how it makes me feel.

Instead, I know that if a space in my home continually gets out of control, there's too much stuff in that space. There is clutter, and I need to declutter that space. If it keeps getting out of control, there's still clutter. I need to keep decluttering until I'm able to keep it under control.

Clutter is anything that gets out of control in *your* home. Clutter is personal. Your Clutter Threshold is why it's personal.

You have a Clutter Threshold, and if your home is usually out of control, you're living above it. Your Clutter Threshold is the amount of stuff that you, personally, can easily keep under control in your own home. If your house is constantly falling back into disaster status, you have too much stuff.

The good news is that once you reach your Clutter Threshold, you'll like your home more. The bad news is that you can only find your Clutter Threshold by decluttering. There's no way to predict what your threshold will be. Solve the problem of your home making you crazy by decluttering. Does it still make you crazy? You need to declutter more. Is it still driving you bananas? Keep decluttering.

> Clutter is anything that gets out of control in *your* home. Clutter is personal.

One day, you'll look around your home and realize, *Wow. My house is staying under control and I no longer feel like I'm hanging off the edge of a cliff by my fingernails.*

You've reached your Clutter Threshold! Congratulations! Now, all you have to do is keep decluttering. If something comes into your home, something else has to leave to make room. That's how you maintain a home that you can keep maintaining.

Strategy 3

EMBRACE LESS AND BETTER

After what felt like millions of failed attempts to "get my act together" in my own house (but was probably only hundreds of thousands), I finally accepted that the way I'd been attempting to change was never going to work.

"Less" and "better" are more effective goals to work toward than "finished" or "done." I love to be done as much as—or more than—anyone. Some of the strategies I'll share later will be all about the power of finishing. But when it came to decluttering my ridiculously cluttered home, the goal of "finishing decluttering" backfired. First of all, it isn't actually possible. Homes that stay clutter-free have people in them who never stop decluttering.

Decluttering success is having less stuff in your house than you did before. This means that even if a space is not finished (perfectly free of clutter), as long as I have removed anything that should not be there, I have successfully decluttered. I'm not done, but there is less. The space is better than it was when I started. Better is good. It's progress. Even if I am sure I won't be able to finish, there is value in making a space better.

Embracing "less" and "better" as valuable goals allows me to start. I am willing to do something, even if I don't have the confidence or time to do the job perfectly.

Focusing on having "less" and making my home "better" is what finally brought about real change in my home. This mindset shift helped me get started, and helps me keep going. Doing something makes my home better—*so much better than it ever was*—simply because there is less.

Strategy 4

JUST DECLUTTER

This book is called *Organizing for the Rest of Us*, but I'm telling you to "just declutter." Decluttering is the secret truly organized people know even though they don't know it's a secret. Decluttering is the missing piece of the puzzle for those of us who have spent our lives trying to get organized, but couldn't.

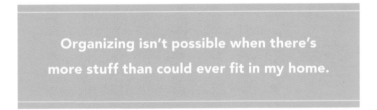

Organizing isn't possible when there's more stuff than could ever fit in my home.

When I started what I call my *deslobification process*, I thought I was giving up when I decided organizing was hopeless for me and I was just going to declutter. Instead, that small but significant change in my thoughts and tactics ultimately changed everything. When I focused exclusively on getting stuff out of my house instead of looking for creative ways to keep my stuff, my home started to look more organized, feel more organized, and function more organized.

I achieved what I'd wanted all along. I had a house that stayed under control. I knew what I had and could find what I needed when I needed it, and I did this by just decluttering.

Organizing and decluttering are two different things. Organizing is problem-solving, and while I'll share some ways to do that, problem-solving can be overwhelming. Organizing isn't possible when there's more stuff than could ever fit in my home.

Give yourself permission (or take my permission) to just declutter; it will give you permission to get started. Remove the stuff that shouldn't be in your home. That alone will solve the vast majority of your frustrations. (Don't worry, I'll give you the steps you need to actually do it.)

STOP TREATING YOUR HOUSE LIKE A PROJECT

I love projects, and I feel competent tackling them. I love planning, executing, and evaluating projects. Because projects are my thing, I treated my house like a project. But that didn't work.

Your house isn't a project, and treating your home like one does more harm than good. There's no beginning, middle, or end. *There's definitely no end.* The project mindset lends itself to putting off starting until there's "time" to really do things right. While you wait for that ideal time, the house gets worse, which means cleaning it up will require even more effort, so you put off starting even longer. It becomes a vicious cycle.

If a top-to-bottom clean ever does happen, celebrating the "big finish" of being done (especially when you're exhausted from working like a maniac) means you want to rest and enjoy your accomplishment.

But dishes keep getting dirty. Trash cans keep filling. Dust falls and toilets get used. I felt like I was "done" after tackling my house like a project, and that was the reason I constantly felt bewildered.

I was looking for a complicated answer to what felt like an incredibly complicated problem, so I couldn't see that the answer was simple. The key to getting your home under control is the little stuff. The "big secret" is not top-to-bottom cleaning every weekend. It's doing the dishes on Monday. And then doing the dishes again on Tuesday, Wednesday, Thursday, Friday, and even . . . on Saturday and Sunday. Even if we went out to eat and the "only" dishes were six cereal bowls, nine spoons, two coffee cups, and a popcorn bowl. The unexciting and nondramatic stuff keeps the house from turning into a project that is procrastination-worthy. Who knew?

Strategy 6

FOLLOW THE VISIBILITY RULE TO
GAIN DECLUTTERING MOMENTUM

When you get the itch to declutter, whether there's a little too much or a lot too much, figuring out where to start can be overwhelming. I learned the hard way that decluttering momentum is best achieved by following the Visibility

Rule. Tackling a rarely used drawer in the garage feels so right, but it's wrong. The work you do in that rarely seen or used space won't inspire you to keep going because you will almost never see or experience the impact of your efforts.

Start decluttering in the most visible area of your home. Not the most cluttered area, the most *visible* area. I recommend starting at your front door, or whichever door guests enter. There's nothing more discouraging in your decluttering journey than working hard all day, but still wanting to hide when the neighbor knocks on your door.

The biggest benefit of following the Visibility Rule, though, is that if you work on a visible space, *you* will see the results of your decluttering effort. While your brain might not have registered the mess, it will register the cleared

space. Every time you walk by this cleared space, you'll feel a little giddy and a lot prouder of yourself for how much better it looks.

Those good feelings will inspire you to declutter more, sooner. Your decluttering energy will increase. Keep going with the next visible space, and you'll gain decluttering momentum.

DECIDE *PROCRASTICLUTTER*
IS WORTH YOUR TIME

*P**rocrasticlutter* is a thing. A very real thing. Procrasticlutter makes many a struggling declutterer moan, "I feel like I'm always decluttering, but my house never looks better!"

Procrasticlutter is the stuff that doesn't seem like legitimate clutter, so it's easy to put off dealing with it when you're in the midst of a "real" decluttering project. (I made up the word, so I get to define it.) You'll have to deal with procrasticlutter eventually, so you know you'll do it eventually. This moment of "I'm finally decluttering right now!" doesn't seem like the right time to deal with that kind of stuff since it isn't "real" clutter.

Examples of procrasticlutter include pile(s) of clean but folded laundry on the recliner(s), clean dishes sitting in the dish drainer, or the stack of papers waiting to be filed in the cabinet it's sitting atop.

Dealing with procrasticlutter feels like stealing time and energy from *real* decluttering.

I had to accept the fact that if I leave piles o' procrasticlutter in a room, whatever work I do in there isn't going to have as obvious an impact. The room will still look messy.

Give yourself permission to deal with procrasticlutter when you declutter, even if doing it frustrates you. Ultimately, you'll have more to show for your effort.

- *Part 2* -

DECLUTTERING BASICS & CURES

(or, at Least, Treatments) for

DECLUTTERING PARALYSIS

Strategy 8

SAY NO TO WHAT YOU THOUGHT DECLUTTERING WAS: STUFF-SHIFTING AND EMOTIONAL DECISIONS

STOP STUFF-SHIFTING

For years, I thought I was decluttering, but I was actually just Stuff Shifting. Coincidentally (or not), those were the same years when I felt forever frustrated that my decluttering efforts didn't have lasting impact.

I wasn't successful because I wasn't removing stuff from my house. I was moving it from one room to another. The core problem of Stuff Shifting is procrastinating on making decisions. I counted on future me to know what to do. I moved things from room to room, usually piling them up, simply because I wanted to keep them.

Don't worry; we'll solve this problem with my decluttering process, but I do want to call you out now on the Stuff Shifting and let you know it's the reason for a lot of your decluttering frustrations. Say no to Stuff Shifting. Begin the decluttering process knowing when you're tempted to stick something in a temporary home "for now," you're not actually decluttering.

I'm more sentimental than the average person. I choose to call this a virtue, but it hasn't served me well in my fight against clutter. I attach emotions to stuff. I let things represent my feelings for the person who gave them to me or the stage of life I was in when I obtained them.

This is why I can't use emotions to declutter. If I assess each item according to how it makes me feel, I will want to keep it. All of it. "Keeping it all" is what caused my house to get out of control.

I remove emotions from my decluttering process by asking fact-based questions that don't allow for long and drawn-out answers. These questions have definitive answers with no agonizing or analyzing required, or even allowed.

You're ready for me to share how I do that, and I'm going to, but I want to make it clear now that decluttering without using emotions is the driving force for the steps in my decluttering process. Letting emotions guide your decluttering is a problem, and my process solves that problem. If you start feeling paralyzed by emotions while you're decluttering, you'll know you're getting off track. If you find yourself staring into space, feeling all the feelings, thinking through all the shoulds and what-ifs, get back to the process.

USE CONTAINERS AS LIMITS:
THE CONTAINER CONCEPT

R eady for the tip that will change everything? The one
that will make everything else make sense? The concept
you didn't know you didn't know but you knew organized
people were born knowing even though you didn't know
what it was?

Containers are limits. That's it. That's everything.

In case you need more, here's more: I used to think containers were for putting things in. I knew organized people

loved them, but when I bought containers and stuck my stuff in them, my house looked junky and nothing like the pictures in the magazines. Then I had a moment. I realized that the root word of *container* is "contain." Like, a container's purpose isn't to hold stuff, it's to contain that stuff. To serve as a limit.

If I put my markers in a bucket, and I have seventy-five markers left over when the bucket is full, I don't need another marker bucket. Instead, I need to let the size of the marker bucket decide how many markers I can keep. When I look at it that way, my brain realizes, "Oh, I guess I don't actually need 125 markers." I don't have to make a value judgment about each marker; I just have to put my favorite markers into the bucket first. Once it's full, I know anything left over has to go.

This frees me because I get to blame the container. Once I realized the purpose of a container was to contain, I accepted that limits were a thing. I don't have to assess the value or future potential usefulness of every item in my house.

The Container Concept transferred to the rest of my house. Just like there was a limit to how many markers could fit in the bucket, there was a limit to how many buckets could fit on a shelf and how many shelves (or shelving units) could fit in a room.

I realized my house is a container. It's finite. I can't shove more in it than will fit, and if I try, the results will be crazy-talk. Every shelf, every sock drawer, every cabinet, every closet, and every basket is a container. Most of all, I realized my family deserves space in the container that is our house more than anything else, so the more stuff I crowd in, the harder it is for my family to function in our home in the way they need to function.

I no longer need to ask myself, "Do I want this?" or "Should I keep this?" I ask, "Does it fit?" Or if I want two things but only have the space for one, I ask, "Which one is container-worthy?"

The Container Concept is simple, and it changes everything.

USE THE RIGHT DECLUTTERING SUPPLIES (AND *ONLY* THOSE SUPPLIES)

This supply list will be the unfanciest decluttering supply list you will see anywhere, but the lack of fanciness is exactly why it works. Fancy tends to equal complicated.

First, you need a black trash bag. This is for . . . trash. The trash bag needs to be black so people in your house can't see what you put inside it. Also, so you can't see what you put inside it.

If you have an established and accessible recycling routine, grab your recycling bin too. If you don't already recycle, stick with the trash bag. The goal is to reduce your clutter and get your house under control so you will have the bandwidth to do the ideal thing. That's what you're working toward, but to get there, you need to get the stuff out, even if that means throwing away trash that could technically be recycled.

Second, you need a donatable Donate Box. Do not, I repeat, *do not* stencil the word *Donate* on the outside of a beautiful container. If you do that, you'll want to keep the container. You would have to transfer your donations into another box to actually donate them. Avoid the extra step. Avoid the possibility of second-guessing your decluttering decisions. If sticking something in your Donate Box means you'll never see it again, you force yourself to make a final decision about each item as you deal with it.

Third, you need feet. They can be your feet or someone else's feet if yours don't work well. Or if you have some sort of transportation device like a scooter or a wheelchair, think of that device when I say feet. For now, I'll just say that your feet are for taking things where they go as soon as you know where they go. If "knowing where things go" stresses you out, relax. That's going to be covered next.

DECLUTTER WITHOUT MAKING
A BIGGER MESS

T he short version of this strategy is this: make a final decision about each item as you pull it out of your cluttered space, and act on that decision immediately.

But I'm not one for short answers.

The number one decluttering frustration is also the number one incorrect assumption about decluttering. It's also the reason people put off decluttering. That frustration/assumption/excuse is that in order to declutter, you first have to make a bigger mess. Or "it has to get worse before it can get better."

That's hogwash. Poppycock. Malarky. Baloney, nonsense, and flat-out untrue. If you read the tip before this one, you know the (completely unfancy) supplies you need. Those supplies (and only those supplies) are what make it possible to declutter without making a bigger mess.

Do not pull everything out of a space. Contrary to what pretty much every other decluttering expert teaches, that is the worst strategy ever. Instead, pull out one item at a time. The steps in my process (coming up after this crucial rule) will guide you through how to do this systematically.

Pulling everything out of a space is exactly what you should do if you live in a perfect world with no interruptions, distractions, or energy limitations (mental, physical, or emotional). I don't live in that kind of world.

When life happened halfway through a decluttering project where I'd pulled everything out of a drawer or closet or an entire room, my house looked worse than it did before I started. Clutter that used to be stuffed behind a cabinet door ended up spread all over my counter. Or on the floor outside my closet.

Remove one item at a time. Make a final decision about each item as you remove it from the space and act on that final decision. Avoid putting anything anywhere temporarily. If something is trash, put it in the trash bag. If you're not keeping it, put it in the Donate Box. If it has a home, put it there. Now.

That last one is the hardest to make yourself do, but it's the key to decluttering without making a bigger mess. Take it there. Right now. Do not make piles of things to put away when you're "done" or put it in a Keep Box. Piles and Keep Boxes seem more efficient, but they are actually just procrastination stations.

When you "take it there now," you can stop at any point, and your space is better off—with less stuff in it than it had when you started. Less stuff equals decluttering success.

FOLLOW THE DECLUTTERING PROCESS
STEP ONE: REMOVE TRASH

A llow me to make a bold statement: my Five-Step Decluttering Process guarantees success. I developed this process by doing the unfun work of decluttering my own home, breaking through my own Decluttering Paralysis, and finding ways to keep going even when I wanted to run away. Follow these steps and you will make progress and will never end up with a bigger mess. That means you can step away at any time and your space will be better off than it was before you started.

Step one of the decluttering process is to *remove trash*. Trash is easy because you don't have to analyze anything. Look for actual trash that makes you roll your eyes instead of breaking your heart.

Identify trash and stick it in your black trash bag. Two things happen when you start with trash. You break through Decluttering Paralysis because you get moving, and you start seeing individual items instead of the overall mass of stuff. Every time something goes into the black trash bag, the overall volume of the mess is reduced, and this reduces your feeling of being overwhelmed.

FOLLOW THE DECLUTTERING PROCESS
STEP TWO: REMOVE THE EASY STUFF

E asy Stuff is the stuff that has an established home somewhere else in your house, but for whatever reason, it isn't
there. Trash was the easiest of the Easy Stuff because it went
straight into the trash bag. Easy Stuff is still easy, but you
may have to walk across the house to take it to its home.
(Or, more likely, turn slightly to your left to put it in its
home eighteen inches from where you found it.)

Look for Easy Stuff, and take it (now) to its home. Every
time you do, the space will be less visually overwhelming
when you return. If you don't return, at least the space will
be better off than it was when you started.

AFTER STEP 2

FOLLOW THE DECLUTTERING PROCESS
STEP THREE: *DUH* CLUTTER

Stick *duh* clutter (or *duhs*) in the Donate Box.

I really do mean *duh* clutter. *Duh* isn't an acronym; it is just the non-word you say when you realize you have something you shouldn't have. The *duh* step gives you permission to stick something in the Donate Box without lamenting the fact that you didn't get rid of the toddler-sized coat three years ago when your kid grew out of it. There's no need to beat yourself up, no need to groan or moan or feel like a failure. *Duhs* happen to everyone. Donate and move on.

It's important to note at this step in the process that once you have purposefully removed trash, Easy Stuff, and *duh* clutter and move on to steps four and five, you're likely to still find trash, Easy Stuff, and *duh* clutter. You have what you need to deal with those, so as you run across them, stick them in the trash, place them in the Donate Box, or walk them to their homes.

AFTER STEP 3

Strategy 15

FOLLOW THE DECLUTTERING PROCESS STEP FOUR: ASK THE TWO DECLUTTERING QUESTIONS

Now that you've removed all (or most of) the angst-free stuff from your cluttered space, start working through it item by item. Pick up something, anything, and ask yourself these two (and only two) questions to make a final decision about that item and put it in its final resting place. The good news is if you can answer question 1, you don't have to ask question 2. Just remember that as you ask the decluttering questions, the answers are instinct-based. If you find yourself hemming and hawing and endlessly analyzing, you're doing it wrong. These questions are designed to work on instinct instead of analysis. Facts instead of feelings. Accept your own answers and be freed by them.

QUESTION 1: *IF I NEEDED THIS ITEM, WHERE WOULD I LOOK FOR IT FIRST?* TAKE IT THERE NOW.

Key words here are *would* and *first*. *Would* is fact-based, so don't accidentally say "should." *Should* opens you up to unending analysis over the very best place to put this thing. *Would* lets you answer immediately and embraces how your family, right now, actually functions.

"First" means you don't need to second-guess yourself. I'm talking about the place in your home where you'd run first if you were frantically looking for this item. If you can answer this first decluttering question, take it there now. That's the key to making progress and never a bigger mess.

QUESTION 2: *IF I NEEDED THIS ITEM, WOULD IT OCCUR TO ME THAT I ALREADY HAD ONE?*

Ask question 2 if (and only if) you didn't have an instinct-based answer to the first question. If you can't answer question 1, that's probably because you wouldn't have looked for it. Be honest with yourself. If you did need this item, would it ever occur to you that you already had one? Would you have even looked, or would you have gone out to buy another one? Or done without?

This is a reality-check question. If the item was a surprise, but you had an answer to question 1, it's in its home. If you didn't have an answer, be honest when you answer this question. If you'd never have looked for it, stick it in the Donate Box. I know this is so hard, but I don't have the word count to answer all your "but, but, buts" in this book. I answered them in *Decluttering at the Speed of Life*, so if you need more words, get that book.

FOLLOW THE DECLUTTERING PROCESS STEP FIVE: MAKE IT FIT

Apply the Container Concept to the space where you're working. At this point, the only stuff left in the space where you're working should be stuff that you'd look for there. But what if the space is still overstuffed?

STEP 5.I: CONSOLIDATE

Put like things together. If you are working on a bookshelf that has books piled horizontally on top of the vertical ones, start by putting like books together. Put Harry Potter together and Baby-Sitter's Club together and cookbooks together.

This step-within-a-step forces you to touch everything. You're still not pulling it all out, but you're consciously moving things. This process often produces more *duhs*. While before, you might have thought, *Books are good and I look for books here*, touching the 1984 low-cal cookbook with a cover picturing a woman in a thong leotard eating meatloaf may awaken the *duh* in your heart. Or maybe you'll realize you have six copies of *Jane Eyre*. Five can go.

Have you noticed that each step of this process is actually about reality acceptance?

You know about the Container Concept. The Container Concept is the ultimate reality acceptance. If the space you're working on is still overfull, start removing things that are less container-worthy. Keep taking out your less favorites until there's only what will fit comfortably and make the space easily usable.

AFTER

Strategy 17

MAINTAIN DECLUTTERING PROGRESS WITH THE ONE-IN-ONE-OUT RULE

The One-In-One-Out Rule is a fact of nature, but it was completely unnatural to me. If I'm going to maintain decluttering progress, if I bring something new into my home, something old has to go.

I had no idea. I've learned that most People Like Me also have no idea. I didn't understand the need to one-in-one-out my stuff because I didn't understand there was a limit to how much stuff I could have in my home if I wanted it to be under control.

I didn't understand the Container Concept. Once I did (the way you hopefully understand now too), one-in-one-outing made total sense.

If the coffee cup I'm using to store pens on my desk is full and I get a new pen (or find my favorite pen under the seat when I clean out my car), I can't just jam the pen I found into the top and let it stick up four inches above all the other pens.

I mean, I *can*. And I did. But that's why my house never looked the way I wanted it to look.

Once I understood the Container Concept, I understood the One-In-One-Out Rule and knew that finding my favorite pen didn't mean my pretty desk was doomed. It just meant I needed to remove my least favorite pen, put that pen in my ongoing-forever-and-ever donatable Donate Box, and *voilà*! The decluttering progress I made on my desk is maintained.

The One-In-One-Out Rule is the key to maintaining all decluttering progress. It keeps your house under your Clutter Threshold and prevents you from sliding backward into clutter.

And it works on more than just pens. It works on sweaters and socks and brooms and vacuum cleaners and yoga mats and water bottles and anything else that comes into your house. It even (and especially) works on furniture.

DON'T LET "VALUE" KEEP YOU
FROM DECLUTTERING

I fell into the trap of viewing my stuff as money. I felt guilty about money I'd wasted, feared spending money to replace something, or dreamed of money I'd make if I sold it.

Perceived or imagined value is a real problem for a lot of us who struggle with clutter. My number one trick for breaking through this roadblock is to give yourself a reality check. You can learn the actual value of an item in minutes.

A quick, two-minute search will eliminate the stumbling block. Look up your item on eBay. (Not that you're necessarily going to sell it on eBay.) This reality check will either spur you to do the work to sell it or give you the freedom to stick it in the Donate Box.

Search specific words that describe your exact item. Is there a stamp on the bottom? A label? What color is it? Look at the pictures that come up in your search, and find the one(s) that look like your treasure. If you need to, reword your search (according to the words in the title of the item that's just like yours) to show you all the items on eBay that are just like yours.

Next comes the most important step: filter the search options to show only completed listings. Completed listings are the only results that matter in your search for reality.

Which items sold, and how much did they sell for? If every single item like yours has sold for an exciting amount of money, great! Did none, or only a rare one, sell?

The value of an item is not the price a hopeful seller asks for it. The value of an item is what someone will pay for it.

Nine times out of ten, this simple internet search will make you willing to get that item (that you don't actually want) out of your house. Sticking nine items in your Donate Box will make your house better.

If you have a room full of stuff you're sure would be worth your time to sell, sell one item. Pick the thing you're most confident will sell. You may decide selling is easy and fun and be motivated to sell more. Or (and this is more likely) you'll learn selling is a lot of stress and effort for less money than you thought, and you'll be ready to donate.

Either way, the stuff will leave your house.

I've decided donation is the way to go, but if I find myself stuck because something is "valuable," I post it in Facebook marketplace, stick it in the Donate Box, and keep working on my decluttering project.

If it hasn't sold by the time I stop decluttering, I remove the listing. In my experience, if something doesn't sell right away, it is unlikely to sell at all. I tried, and I can move on.

TAKE A BEFORE PHOTO

My five-step decluttering process is designed to cure your decluttering paralysis by starting with the least overwhelming tasks and letting you see visible progress immediately. That will inspire you to keep going. Follow the process, and you'll make an impact on your home.

I'm going to share a few additional tips for busting through your Decluttering Paralysis, though, since I know that those of us who tend to be overwhelmed by clutter can easily get stuck along the way.

I have to force myself to take before photos, but every time I do, I'm so glad; and every time I don't take one, I wish I had.

When you are overwhelmed and convinced there's no

decluttering hope for you, it is very hard to make yourself take a photo of the space you want to declutter, but do it anyway. Or take a photo of a small portion of the space you want to declutter, one shelf or one drawer or one corner.

Set a timer for five minutes, and when the timer goes off, take another picture. Start the decluttering process by throwing away trash. That's step one. Swipe back and forth between the photos and show yourself what can be done in just five minutes of throwing away trash. You'll be surprised at the impact of five minutes of my progress (and only progress) no-mess decluttering method.

Hopefully, you'll keep going after the five minutes, but take another photo whenever you stop. If you're using your smartphone, you'll have time stamps and visual proof of exactly how much you can accomplish. That proof will go far in curing your Decluttering Paralysis.

> You'll be surprised at the impact of five minutes of my progress—and only progress—no-mess decluttering method.

TIME YOUR TASKS

Time yourself doing the thing you put off doing. Get a reality-based understanding of how long it takes to do this thing instead of letting your mind exaggerate.

My best example of the impact of timing a dreaded task is emptying the dishwasher. I would have thought, claimed, and possibly even fought with you that emptying my dishwasher took at least fifteen to twenty minutes. It doesn't. It takes me about four minutes.

Once I knew this for a fact, it was harder to justify not emptying my dishwasher when I have four minutes available. Knowing for a fact how long it takes to do something removes so many excuses for not doing it.

Other ideas of tasks to time are folding and putting away a load of laundry, handwashing a day's worth of dishes, sweeping the kitchen, or scrubbing a toilet.

DON'T FEEL GUILTY ABOUT
BREAKING UP SETS

My friend Dawn, of the YouTube channel *The Minimal Mom*, always reminds people that it is perfectly fine to break up sets. I love this tip.

Ultimately it's a mindset that means I am not obligated to keep anything in my home that I don't want to keep in my home. It can be as simple as letting go of the yellow marker from a set my daughter bought to write in her journal. If she doesn't want to use the yellow marker, she can let the yellow marker go.

Or it can be the weirdly sized skillet from a twenty-piece set of pots and pans! The people selling the pots and pans wanted to be able to count twenty pieces, but if you won't use that size skillet, donate it.

Strategy 22

FINISH A PROJECT AND CALL
IT DECLUTTERING

For creative people, a lot of clutter happens because of unfinished projects. Parts and pieces that haven't been put together need somewhere to go, and many times the most

logical somewhere is on the surface where you started the project. To put the unfinished project away in a cabinet feels wrong—because how are you ever supposed to finish it then?

I'm here to declare that finishing a project counts as decluttering. If the supplies are in limbo, covering a surface that needs to be used for something else, that's clutter.

If the project is finished, it can now go to its final resting place, its home within your home. At that point, it isn't clutter. Finish the project. Call that decluttering.

Also, if you give yourself permission to finish the project so it won't be clutter, and you then realize you don't actually *want* to finish the project, you'll be able to let the pieces go. Either way, no heads will have exploded. That's good.

FOLLOW THE HEAD-EXPLOSION RULE

I made up a rule that has saved me many times. I hear from people regularly who love this rule too. I call it the Head-Explosion Rule. If an item makes my brain hurt, if I can't stop going back and forth between the reasons I might use it and the reasons I don't actually want it in my house, until my head feels like it's going to explode, I declutter it.

No item is worth my head exploding, so it needs to go.

- Part 3 -

The

CONTAINER CONCEPT

and

RETHINKING STORAGE

CONTAIN STUFFED ANIMALS

T he Container Concept changed everything for me. About 99 percent of my answers to questions about decluttering start with, "Well, it all boils down to the Container Concept." Grasp this concept, and you will go far.

Stuffed animals are cute, cuddly, and some kids end up with gazillions of them. The Container Concept works, even when it feels like there couldn't possibly be a limit because you love them all.

If I love them all, they all have value. How could I choose which should go? The Container Concept lets you flip the script. Instead of asking which stuffed animal you like least, ask which is your favorite.

Designate a container with clear boundaries. A shelf works as well as a plastic tub. Remember that the room is also a container and needs to hold the stuffed-animal container (and other containers) as well as allow space to sleep, play, and live. (I'm starting with a kid's scenario since it's easier to see the logic when talking about someone else's stuff. We'll get to your stuff next.)

You've probably collected storage solutions, so use what you have. The concept is more important than the container.

Show your child the special place for stuffed animals. Ask him to put his favorite one in first. Then the next favorite, and the next. As he's picking favorites, casually mention that once the container is full, the rest will go in the Donate Box.

This process naturally sorts out the most loved things, and the size of the container determines how many your child can keep. The container is the bad guy. You get to be sympathetic.

If your child wants to keep a stuffed animal that doesn't fit, they can keep it! All they have to do is choose which animal to remove so there's room. If this makes them sad, hold them close and be sad together.

If one container isn't enough, say, "Of course you can keep more! What do you want to donate so you can free up another container? LEGOs? Hot Wheels?" They decide what stays and goes, and you get to blame the container. Reality is hard. Limits make sense, even to kids.

CONTAIN YOUR SOCK DRAWER

One question I hear a lot, and that I personally had when I was overwhelmed by clothing was, "How many socks/ shoes/undies/jeans/headbands/whatever should I keep?" It's tempting, especially with clothing, to sit down and start doing math instead of grabbing the Donate Box.

There's no need for math. The question is not "How many socks do I need?" but "How big is my sock drawer?" If your sock drawer won't close easily, you have too many socks. Remove your least favorite socks until the drawer

closes smoothly and you can get to the socks you want without causing a mess.

If you get a new pair of warm and fuzzy socks, and your sock drawer is full, all you have to do is one-in-one-out to make room for your new pair of socks.

Which pair do you like less than the new pair you just bought? Usually, asking yourself this question is easy. You immediately identify the pair that always slips down into your boot. Get rid of that one to make room for the new ones you want to keep.

If you love socks, fine. But the size of the drawer is the size of the drawer, and the number of drawers in the dresser is the number of drawers in the dresser. You can dedicate a second drawer to socks, but that means you will have to give up whatever is in that drawer. Are you willing to have fewer T-shirts to keep more socks?

If you're tempted to buy a second dresser so you can keep all the socks and all the T-shirts, consider the size of the room. The size of the room is the size of the room, and you need to be able to move around and do what you need to do in that room without bumping into things. What are you willing to get rid of to make room for the new dresser?

Let the container be the bad guy. Let the container be the limit. I promise it's easier than stubbed toes and bruised hips from bumping into the extra chest of drawers that doesn't fit in the room.

You can keep anything. You just can't keep everything.

CONTAIN YOUR COFFEE MUGS

L et's apply the Container Concept to coffee mugs. They're easy to collect from souvenir shops and they come into the house as gifts. So, like stuffed animals, coffee cups can be highly sentimental.

But they also have the extra appeal of being . . . useful. My husband and I drink coffee every single day. Two of our teenagers drink it some days. My husband loves to brew a pot when we have guests. Like with socks, it's tempting to start doing math to figure out how many coffee cups we should have in our home.

Instead, it's much easier and effective and my house is better off if I just apply the Container Concept to our coffee mugs.

We have one small cabinet shelf for coffee cups, and that's where we have always kept them in this house. Before I understood that every space in my home is a container and needs to serve as a limit to how much stuff I can keep, we pushed and shoved and piled coffee cups on top of one another in that cabinet.

But once I understood that that shelf was a container,

I was free to look at my coffee cups differently. Instead of stressing over how to store them, I gave myself permission to let some go. I didn't need to do math; I just needed to accept the size of the shelf as the limit to how many coffee cups I can keep.

I got rid of the ones that were ugly, the ones that didn't hold enough or held too much. I got rid of the ones that were freebies from companies we had never heard of other than reading their names on our coffee cups.

Once I only had as many coffee cups as fit easily on that shelf, I could see what I had and get to what I wanted more easily. And when I remembered that our two favorite coffee cups were in the dishwasher, I didn't despair (like I used to do); I just took out the two we liked least to make room for the two we liked most.

Just like with the socks, accepting the shelf as the limit for coffee cups freed me to let go of coffee cups. It helped my brain accept, simply and without angst, that we didn't actually need as many coffee cups as we'd been trying to keep. They're always useful and they're often sentimental, but we can't keep them all. There simply isn't space.

CREATE A KEEPSAKE BOX

I'm anti–Keep Box. I'm not anti-Keepsake Box. A Keep Box is a box where you put stuff to deal with later. Don't do that. That's a procrastination station.

But a Keepsake Box is a beautiful thing. It's a container whose purpose is to contain things you want to keep that serve no purpose other than to be a memory.

Just always remember that it is a container. A limit. If you don't have a Keepsake Box, don't decide on a size to get according to how much stuff you think you will want to keep for the sake of memories. Instead, decide what space you have available to store the box. Choose a space you aren't using for anything you need to live life right now, since right-now living always has to come first. Maybe it's a part of a

> A Keep Box is a box where you put stuff to deal with later. Don't do that. That's a procrastination station.

shelf in your closet. Maybe it's under your bed. Choose a box that will fit in that space. It doesn't need to be fancy; it just needs to be limited.

As you declutter, if you find something that should go into a Donate Box according to the decluttering process because it doesn't have a home, but you absolutely cannot bear to get rid of it, put it in your Keepsake Box. Just know that the box is the limit to how many of these kinds of things you can keep. When the Keepsake Box is full, it's full; if you want to put something new in it, something else will have to leave to create space for the thing you want to keep.

CONTAIN LOVED ONES' STUFF

I hope that by now you're starting to see how you can apply the Container Concept in every space in your home. It is the ultimate answer to all your decluttering woes.

Even the hardest, most sentimental ones.

Like Grandma's rocking chair. While everything in Grandma's house feels sentimental, it isn't physically possible to bring all her furniture into your house without your house (full of your existing furniture) turning into a jumbled mess.

So you one-in-one-out. And one-in-one-outing Grandma's rocking chair doesn't have to mean you get rid of another chair. You just have to get rid of something (or some things) that will open up the space you need for Grandma's rocking chair.

One-in-one-outing isn't item for item; it's space for space. Maybe the plant stand that felt like a good idea but has only ever held the decaying remains of a fiddle-leaf fig can go. Its departure will create the space you need for Grandma's rocking chair. Your home will be better for bringing in this sentimental chair.

Or you may look at your beautiful space and realize

there isn't anything you're willing to give up to make space for Grandma's rocking chair. Maybe you worked hard to buy furniture and arrange your living room just so. Maybe you love rocking your own babies in the chair you chose when your oldest was born, and Grandma's chair isn't nearly as comfortable as that one. You can't keep Grandma's rocking chair. Blame the container. Blame the limitations of your space. You love the chair and you loved Grandma. Take a photo of you sitting in it and donate the chair so someone can enjoy it. That's a much more pleasant option than grunting in frustration as you bump into it six times a day for the next thirty years.

The space made the decision. Not keeping Grandma's rocking chair doesn't mean you don't value it. It just means you don't have room for it.

FIND STORAGE SPACE, DON'T ADD IT

I used to daydream about houses with basements. I loved my grandparents' basement in Kansas, but basements don't exist in my part of Texas. Surely, if I had a basement, all my clutter problems would be solved. All. That. Space.

Storage space feels like it should be magical. Yet with every move to a bigger home, my clutter issues never went away.

When you're overwhelmed by the amount of stuff in your home, it is tempting to search the term *storage solutions*.

Or to call a contractor to ask how much it would cost to build a shed in your backyard or add a room to your house.

But if you just got it through your head in the last section that your house is a container, you probably know I'm not going to tell you how to add storage space or bring in new storage solutions.

My advice is to find storage space in your house. If you have a corner that is piled with supplies to make baskets, and you actually make baskets, those supplies deserve a dedicated storage space in your home. Find the space to store them by identifying and decluttering a space that is filled with things you don't use.

This is the Container Concept in action. In a home that's under control, there aren't piles of basket-making supplies in the corner of the dining room. (Sorry.)

What is being stored in your home that doesn't deserve space as much as the basket-making supplies? Start looking in natural storage spaces (cabinets, closets) near where you make baskets. Most likely, you will find that you have been storing something you don't like as much as you like making baskets. Maybe it's supplies for making wreaths even though you stopped making wreaths when you started making baskets.

Prioritize the hobby you're into right now over the hobby you were into last year or the memories you brought home from your mother's house.

Don't add storage. Find storage in your house.

PRIORITIZE "GET-TO-ABILITY"
IN ANY STORAGE SPACE

Storage spaces can be a topic of heated debate among declutterers. It's kind of an existential question. I'm not going to tell you to never store things. I will tell you to focus on *get-to-ability*. Or, if you are into real words, *accessibility*.

How you'll get to something needs to be the deciding factor in how you store it.

If you enjoy the process of creating a complicated puzzle of stored stuff, *and* you consistently follow through with putting everything back perfectly after you get out the thing you need, go for it. Create your own Jenga in your storage spaces.

If you're not giddy about arranging and rearranging, you have a lower Clutter Threshold. Store things where you can see them and get to them easily. There needs to be open space around things, which means you store less.

Sometimes, just asking the question about whether this thing will be get-to-able will help you realize you don't actually care about getting to it, which will help you realize you don't actually care about keeping it.

USE PEGBOARDS

I am a huge fan of the pegboards that cover the walls in my garage. Pegboards allow me to store things where I can see them, unpiled. I can hang lawn tools and tennis rackets and bike helmets right on the wall.

If we ever move, I'll definitely install pegboards in our new garage.

Collect a variety of lengths of pegs, and get doubles of all that you buy. Two of the same length of peg used together allows you to hang things that are a little heavier.

AVOID MISCELLANEOUS STORAGE

Whether you are talking about boxes on shelves in your garage or bins for small toys in your kid's bedroom, avoid labeling any container as "miscellaneous."

I know it's hard. A box marked Miscellaneous feels necessary. It feels safe. Where else are you supposed to put all the random leftovers once the space is organized?

But "miscellaneous storage" is basically an excuse to keep things that don't have an actual home. The temptation to throw something into a box marked Miscellaneous is too strong and lets me avoid forcing myself to answer the decluttering questions.

You may go slower, but your progress will be real and lasting if you force yourself to avoid miscellaneous storage.

CHOOSE ORGANIZING PRODUCTS
AFTER YOU DECLUTTER

I understand the allure of the pretty pictures of aspirational spaces on organizing product packaging. But they lie.

Declutter your space first, and then live with that space for a while. You'll be amazed at how much more usable your space is and how much more organized it feels simply by removing the stuff that shouldn't be there and living within its limits.

So many times, after decluttering a space, I realize I never actually needed any fancy organizing products. I just needed to be able to see and get to my stuff without a bunch of clutter in my way.

But even if I do need organizing products, the best way to figure out the right ones (bins, baskets, tubs, whatever) is to live with my decluttered space for a while. After I live with a space that only has what should actually be there, I can see clearly that a basket here or a bin there will help me maintain it the way it needs to be maintained. Even then, try out your solution with a box you already have that feels like it is the size you'll need. It may not be beautiful, but living with that no-cost solution for a while will help you know for sure what will work before you spend money and bring something into your house that will have to be decluttered if it doesn't work.

- Part 4 -

CLEANING ROUTINES

and

EASILY FORGOTTEN CLEANING TASKS

Strategy 33

IMPLEMENT DAILY TASKS

Daily tasks and decluttering go hand-in-hand. Daily tasks will reveal what you can declutter, and decluttering will make it easier to keep up with your daily tasks.

I'm going to teach you which four daily tasks I've learned, from experience, will take anyone from feeling completely overwhelmed to being confident she can get her home (and keep her home) under control. Once you know what these four tasks are and experience their surprising impact, you'll have a path to get back on when things get wonky again. Things *will* get wonky again.

But before I share what they are, I do have some bad news. Daily tasks are work. I thought when people talked about making it a "habit" to do their dishes every day, or the "habit" of doing a daily pickup, they meant habits like my bad habits that I do without realizing I am doing them.

I always realize I'm doing the dishes. I often feel irritated about doing them and have to verbally talk myself into doing them.

But while I never exclaim, "Wait! Did I just clean my kitchen? I guess I did!" daily tasks do get easier the more I do them. They build. If I do something every day, the problem I'm dealing with only has twenty-four-ish hours to build instead of a week or a month. Daily tasks also get easier because they stop feeling unnatural. I know where to find the supplies I need and I know where to start. Daily tasks also get easier to make myself do because I learn from experience that they make life easier to live.

As daily tasks become easier to do, I free up time. That helps me declutter more. Decluttering more makes it easier to do my daily tasks.

Here is *how* I came up with these four daily tasks. I picked the problem in my home that drove me craziest, and I solved it. Then (and here's the key), I solved the same problem again the next day. And again the next day. In my experience, after seven days, I figured out how to keep the problem from recurring in my home.

Maybe you already have these four tasks under control. Maybe you don't like someone telling you what to do, and you want to figure it out on your own.

Solve your most annoying problem today, then solve it again tomorrow. After seven days, you'll have figured out a routine that works in your home, for your lifestyle, that will keep that problem from being a problem.

DO YOUR DISHES EVERY SINGLE DAY

Dishes are the very least you can do and the very first thing you should do. If you don't do your dishes, you won't have plates when you need to eat. If you find a clean pasta pot, you won't have room in the sink to drain spaghetti because it will be full of dirty dishes.

Life screeches to a halt when you don't do your dishes. If you don't make your bed in the morning, you can still go to bed that night. You might have to tug a little harder on your blankets, but nothing becomes impossible if you don't make your bed.

When I was completely overwhelmed, I needed to know what *actually* mattered most. What did I absolutely *have* to do?

When someone told me to start by making my bed, and I knew (from a lifetime of experience) that an unmade bed didn't keep me from being able to sleep at night, I could tell we weren't speaking the same language. I knew they didn't actually understand my question or my starting point.

I'm telling you the thing that is so obvious to most of the people who write about this stuff that they don't know there are people who need to be told.

Do your dishes. Every single day.

I run my dishwasher after dinner, whether I think I have enough dirty dishes to fill it or not. Loading my dishwasher shows me (90 percent of the time) that I did, in fact, have enough dirty dishes to fill it.

Loading my dishwasher means I notice the dish(es) on the far end of the counter. It means I (am more likely to) walk through my house looking for random dishes.

Running my dishwasher every single evening means there is usually room for my pots and pans too. Not hand-washing makes me happy.

Your schedule may be different and your situation may be different, but at some point, every single day, your dishes need to be done.

When you figure out your personal "every single day" point, something will shift in how you see your dishes. You'll have a finish line.

When you have a Dishes Finish Line, a single dish doesn't look like the beginning of a pile; it looks like an easy thing to do that will move you a little closer to your finish line.

ACCEPT DISHES MATH

ONE DAY'S WORTH OF DISHES

Dishes Math is a real thing, and accepting it as fact will eliminate your resistance to doing your dishes every day.

Dishes Math works like this: One day's worth of dishes takes ten to fifteen minutes to do. Two days' worth of dishes takes an hour because the sink is already full from yesterday, and you have to rearrange things to get them all done or run two loads of the dishwasher.

Three days' (or more) worth of dishes takes hours to do. You can't leave everything in a dish drainer to dry; you have to dry the dishes and put them away so you have room to wash yet another load. This means more work and *so* much more time.

Understanding Dishes Math motivates me to do my dishes every single day. It's what helps me understand the difference between "doing the dishes" being quick and easy and "doing the dishes" being daunting and exhausting.

TWO DAYS' WORTH OF DISHES

THREE DAYS' WORTH OF DISHES

I used to resist doing my dishes every single day because I'd only ever experienced three-day-or-more dishes. I thought doing the dishes was a big, intensive project because that was all I knew. The experience of doing only one day's worth of dishes was shocking.

One day's worth takes only ten to fifteen minutes? I honestly didn't know.

RUN YOUR DISHWASHER
EVEN IF IT ISN'T FULL

H ere's a tip that will make some people's undies get super wadded up superfast.

Run your dishwasher every single day, even if it isn't completely full. Do the research. I learned when I visited the Maytag labs and talked to the engineers who design them that dishwashers use significantly less water than handwashing. We were told that on average, the water used to handwash a dish is three times the liquid capacity of that dish. According to NRDC.org, "You use up to 27 gallons of water per load by hand versus as little as 3 gallons with an ENERGY STAR-rated dishwasher." That's a lot less water.

In most households, not running the dishwasher will result in more than a dishwasher-full on the second day. At that point, your choice will be between handwashing the extra (using more water than if you'd run two not-completely-full loads in the dishwasher) or getting off routine and getting behind.

FOCUS ON THE ROUTINE (AND NOT YOUR LACK OF—OR LOUSY—DISHWASHER)

If you don't have a dishwasher, I'm sorry. I know your response (if you're funny) is to say, "But I *am* the dishwasher!" If you're not funny, you're mad at me.

Here's the truth. If you don't have a dishwasher, you don't have a dishwasher. None of these tips are actually about the dishwasher. They are about the routine of getting the dishes done.

The dishwasher helps, but it's not magic. There are plenty of people in the world who don't have dishwashers but their kitchens stay clean because they have a dishes routine. They have a finish line for their dishes.

There are plenty of people in the world who have dishwashers (even top-of-the-line, super-fancy ones), whose kitchens are total disasters, and many of them are reading this book.

Do your dishes every night before you go to bed. Make that your finish line until you end up realizing (because you've been doing your dishes every night) that a different time of day is a better Dishes Finish Line for you.

Experience Dishes Math. Do your dishes today, and then do them again tomorrow. Experience the difference in time required. Then, do your dishes again the next day and the next and the next to keep proving to yourself that doing one day's worth of dishes isn't nearly as big of a deal as you assumed it was back when you used to put off doing your dishes.

SWEEP THE KITCHEN EVERY DAY

Sweeping the kitchen every day isn't about maintaining a crumb-free kitchen floor. A briefly crumb-free kitchen floor is a perk of this daily task, but it isn't the point.

The point of sweeping the kitchen every day is to give myself a daily reality check. I have an amazing ability to avoid reality. My brain chooses not to register daily annoyances because it's focused on other things.

That's a great quality, y'all. It's the thing that helps me get big things done. Things like writing books or organizing meals for fifty kids at a weekend retreat.

But it's also the thing that causes me to ignore little "unimportant" things like newspapers or grocery bags full of canned goods sitting on the kitchen floor because they never got put away.

Sweeping the kitchen every day isn't about crumbs. It's about open-ing my eyes to random things that need to be picked up or straightened on my kitchen floor. It's not fun, but it's necessary for me, as someone who doesn't notice crumbs *or* grocery bags.

I don't see incremental mess. I see perfectly neat and I see overwhelmingly messy. The in-between is invisible to me. Daily tasks like sweeping the floor are about dealing with the incremental mess so it doesn't become overwhelming.

The good news is that just like doing the dishes, sweeping the kitchen floor is significantly easier on the second day and every day after that. Don't assume you know that "sweeping your kitchen" is an hours-long task. The first day might take a long time because it may include decluttering the corner where you've been piling random stuff. The first day might include collecting all the toys or hair barrettes or shoes that have been collecting on your kitchen floor for who knows how long. There may be toys or hair barrettes tomorrow, but tomorrow it will only be one day's worth, and that will be easier.

If your dishes are done every day (so your counters and table are clear) and your floors are swept, your kitchen is going to look pretty good. Especially compared to what it used to look like when you weren't doing your dishes every day and hadn't swept your kitchen since the last time your mother-in-law visited.

CHECK THE BATHROOMS FOR CLUTTER

Like sweeping the kitchen every day, this daily task is a reality check.

Check your bathrooms for clutter every day. Clutter might be toothbrushes placed on the counter a half-inch from the toothbrush holder. It might be dirty clothes on the floor. It might be empty toilet paper rolls hiding behind the toilet. It might be three empty shampoo bottles sitting upside-down beside the full one.

Like the two previous daily tasks, checking the bathrooms for clutter will take the longest to accomplish on the first day. The first day will involve actual decluttering. You'll have to go through the buildup of weeks or months or even years of random things being placed in random places. My gift to you is that you don't need to declutter deep into the drawers and cabinets. That will happen when you do "real" decluttering as opposed to this daily task.

After the first day, this task becomes a quick check instead of a cleanup. You'll purposefully look. You'll see the single pair of undies on the floor or the single hairbrush on the edge of the bathtub, and you'll deal with that. And you'll be done.

These bathroom checks take very little time, but they are important. If you keep this oft-used space from collecting piles of randomness, that means you could wipe things down quickly if you wanted to. If you found out someone was coming over, or if a friend knocked on your door begging for a potty for her three-year-old, you could wipe the sink and toilet in less than a minute and be ready to let them use your bathroom without having a panic attack. You can do this because you don't have to move things or rearrange things or deal with anything first. You can *just* wipe it down.

And when it's time to clean your bathroom, you *just* have to clean the bathroom. That means you'll be 1,000 percent less likely to come up with a reason to put off cleaning your bathroom.

DO A DAILY FIVE-MINUTE PICKUP

People whose homes are generally under control do daily pickups. Maybe they naturally put scissors away instead of unconsciously setting them down in random places (like I do). Maybe they set an alarm or just remember toys and assorted randomness should be picked up and put away before bedtime.

I knew daily pickups were key to avoiding disaster status, but I never felt like I could implement them in my home. The first day of this task was always so daunting that I gave up. I was making up for months of not doing daily pickups, so in order to do this "right," I'd be up all night. I picked the smallest amount of time I could justify for a daily pickup: five minutes. Unlike the other three daily tasks, I didn't catch up on the first day.

Let the five-minute pickups build. Every time you do a five-minute pickup, you'll put more stuff away. The first day will make an impact, and each day will increase that impact. When you get to the point that five minutes gets your house (mostly) back under control, you've hit your clutter threshold.

- Don't designate a specific time of day to do a five-minute pickup. When I realize I need to do a five-minute pickup, I *do* it right then, and my house improves. If I remember to do another one at bedtime, there will always be more to pick up. But my house is better off if I don't assign this task to a specific time I might miss.

- The five-minute pickup is the best daily task for involving the entire family, even right from the beginning (if they're home when you think of doing one). It won't be *fun* the first two or sixteen times, but keep going. A family of five doing a five-minute pickup will have twenty-five minutes' worth of impact on your home. That's math, y'all.

- Stop after five minutes. I don't like to be tricked, so I don't try to trick myself into doing thirty minutes by telling myself I only have to do five. Your family doesn't like to be tricked either. Knowing you mean five minutes will significantly decrease resistance to this daily (or almost daily) task.

- Rule out pooping during the five-minute pickup. Every family has a pooper procrastinator.

PUT CLEANING ON THE (TOTALLY ADJUSTABLE) SCHEDULE

We are down to the final layer of a clean house: actual cleaning. I assign major cleaning tasks to specific days of the week. Laundry on Mondays. Bathrooms on Tuesdays. Errands on Wednesdays, mopping on Thursdays, and dusting/vacuuming on Fridays.

If a week goes perfectly, major cleaning tasks get done. But even though weeks rarely go perfectly, this routine still works. If I can't or *don't* clean bathrooms on Tuesday, I don't switch up the entire week. I acknowledge life happens. My bathroom doesn't look *that* bad because dealing with surface clutter is a daily task. I can do a quick wipe down if needed, and Tuesday will come around again next week. If I'm looking for an excuse to avoid cleaning bathrooms, realizing I missed the last two Tuesdays is a natural reality check.

Routine is how I fight my TPAD, especially when it comes to cleaning. TPAD is short for a term I made up: Time Passage Awareness Disorder. It means I struggle to have any awareness of how long it has been since I last did something, especially something I don't want to do. Like cleaning.

If your schedule doesn't allow you to do one task a day, find another regularly occurring natural reminder that works in your life. Maybe you clean for an hour before movie night, or first and third Saturdays each month works for you.

If you're scared, establish a time limit. Saying you're going to "clean the house" is overwhelming if you've only ever done catch-up cleaning. A time limit ensures there's an end. You imagine you need seventeen hours to clean your shower, but you're giving yourself permission to work for two hours total on your house. Divide those two hours up by tasks. Devote forty minutes to cleaning bathrooms, twenty minutes to dusting as much as you can, thirty minutes to mopping the kitchen, and thirty minutes to vacuuming.

A time limit lets you start because you know you'll get to stop, and your house will be better off for the work you do. You'll clean more—even with an imperfect routine— than if you don't have a routine. And don't forget: if you're keeping up with the first two layers (daily stuff and decluttering), "real" cleaning won't feel (as) daunting. Mopping the kitchen won't mean clearing debris. It will just mean mopping. Cleaning will go faster and be easier so you'll be less likely to procrastinate when your routine reminds you it's time to clean.

TRY LAUNDRY DAY

I f you never worry about having clean undies, skip this tip. If you do wonder about undies, try Laundry Day. Most "experts" tell you to do one load each day. If that works for you, great. But also, why are you still reading this tip?

Some people cannot keep up with laundry by doing one load a day. I am one of those people. I wash a load but forget to move it to the dryer. When I remember, the clothes smell funny and I have to rewash them.

I tried. I wrote notes and set timers. Nothing worked. Finally, I tried Laundry Day, and it worked for me. It also works for thousands of others whose brains work like mine.

HOW DOES LAUNDRY DAY WORK?

Sort every piece of dirty laundry (from your entire house) into piles. I do this in a hallway. Work through the piles. When one load finishes drying, fold and put those clothes away immediately, then move the load in the washer to the dryer. Wash the next load. By the end of the day, for most households, all your laundry will be done for the week.

Wait! Before you throw this book across the room, keep reading. I know it's not that simple. I know your ~~excuses~~ reasons why this won't work. I answered *all* of them in *How to Manage Your Home Without Losing Your Mind*. I won't re-answer them here, but I will show you there is hope if you will give it three weeks.

LAUNDRY DAY #1

On Laundry Day #1, you'll be mad because there's *so much laundry*. You're catching up from being behind for the last who knows how long. The good news: only worry about the clothes you gathered. All newly dirtied laundry goes into hampers. That's next week's laundry. The bad news: finishing Laundry Day #1 may take a week.

On Laundry Day #2, you'll be mad because you *just* finished Laundry Day #1. But starting again will be worth it. You'll know, for real, what one week's worth of laundry is in your home. Laundry Day #1 was no indication.

LAUNDRY DAY #2

The magic happens on Laundry Day #3, but it can only happen if you get through Laundry Day #2. For my family of five adult-sized people, I can finish in one day with four to six loads. I like to put in the first load the night before so I get a head start. Immediately after Laundry Day #2, the magic of Laundry Day #3 begins. The magic is that between laundry days, you have six days without laundry guilt, without even needing to think about laundry.

You'll be done, and your family will have all the underwear and socks and T-shirts they need. Don't underestimate the impact on your stress levels of being done with laundry.

LOOK FOR—AND USE—AWKWARD PAUSES

One big perk of identifying which daily tasks are most important is that you know what to do when you experience an awkward pause. Awkward pauses are those moments in your day when you have a small and unexpected amount of unscheduled time between things you have to do. Knowing what to focus on in those moments is huge.

If you have a Dishes Finish Line, using a two-minute pause to put random dishes into the dishwasher feels satisfying because you're getting ahead on your goal; it won't feel pointless because you can't "do it properly."

A five-minute pause is enough to check off your five-minute pickup for the day. When you know which tasks have the highest impact, you can spend awkward pauses getting things done instead of feeling overwhelmed by how much you have to do and how little time you have to do it.

With the no-mess decluttering method, you can declutter for three minutes, or even two. Throw trash away. Look for Easy Stuff in the pile on the dining room table.

Five minutes matter. Three minutes matter. There's a lot of value in awkward pauses. Using them well will take you far.

Strategy 44

CLEAN YOUR DOORKNOBS
AND LIGHT SWITCHES

A friend once told me that her fear in inviting people into her home was that she would have completely missed cleaning something that everyone but her knew should be cleaned. I'm here to tell you that I'm sure I've forgotten to clean some very important things. Most people (at least the ones you want to come back) aren't going to stop being your friends because you missed cleaning something. They just want to be invited over and they want to spend time with you. But to make you feel better, here are a few cleaning tasks that are easily forgotten (or completely missed) that can have a big impact on how clean a house looks and feels.

\- - -

I'm fanatical about washing my hands, so I'm always shocked at the level of grime that ends up around doorknobs and light switches. I don't understand how it happens, and I don't understand how I can go so long without noticing it, only to suddenly realize that the area looks absolutely disgusting.

Grab a damp (not wet since we're dealing with light switches) microfiber cloth, a cleaning wipe, or (my personal favorite for this job) a Magic Eraser, and walk through your house cleaning doorknobs, light switches, and the wall surfaces around them. Just don't be surprised if you end up cleaning entire doors.

Pay close attention to the inside of the door of the bathroom your guests use. If you leave your bathroom door open when it isn't being used, you may pay no attention to this side of the door, but a guest with, ummm, nothing else to do while they're sitting in there doesn't need to have grime and random splatters (*blech*) to contemplate.

DUST THE FORGOTTEN PLACES

VACUUM WINDOWSILLS

Windowsills can be the grossest places to dust because they tend to be graveyards for bugs. Also, they're easy to ignore behind curtains or blinds so they end up with quite a bit of dirt and grime and cobwebs. I'm a big fan of using a handheld vacuum or the attachments on a vacuum cleaner to suck away as much of the dust and cobwebs as possible before I use my other dusting methods. That's so much more effective than just swiping at it. Vacuuming first lets you avoid the mess that happens if you spray a highly dusty space with a liquid that turns the dust into mud. (Dust is dirt, y'know.)

DUST HIGH-UP, HIDDEN SURFACES

I hate dusting spots that no one ever sees, but I also hate being grossed out when I do happen to see those spots (like the top of my refrigerator or the tops of kitchen cabinets) and they're covered in thick dust. And then I think about all the tall people who've walked through our house.

But if I line the unseen-anyway space with paper towels, all I have to do is remove the paper towel and replace it, with no actual cleaning needed.

DUST THE WALLS

I'm so sorry to be the one to tell you this, but being a grownup means dusting your walls. I don't like it either. I avoid dusting walls for as long as I possibly can. But, when I start whining to myself (or others) that my house just doesn't feeeeel cleeeeeaaannn, I usually need to dust my walls.

Dusting walls is irritating, because dust shouldn't be allowed to settle on walls, but it settles there anyway. You can dust walls with whatever you use to do a quick dusting of your floors. Swiffers, microfiber dry mops, or whatever you have will work just fine.

Strategy 46

CLEAN THE BATHROOM MIRROR
AFTER YOU SHOWER

Some people see toothpaste splatter every time it splatters. Some people (like me) don't. To make it an easy fix instead of a big cleaning project, keep a microfiber cloth in the bathroom, and after a steamy shower use the cloth to wipe down the already steamy mirrors. This will remove the vast majority of toothpaste splatters and random water spots.

- Part 5 -

PROCRASTINATION STATION ELIMINATION

DON'T FALL FOR THE SOAKING TRAP

I've got procrastination skills. I can argue the case for avoiding something I don't want to do like nobody's business. But eventually I had to stop myself. My natural talent for justifying procrastination was making my house a disaster zone.

I have identified many tasks that are simpler and less time-consuming if I'll just go ahead and do them. I'm going to tell you about a few.

But first I'm going to say something that many of you will not like. Soaking is a sham. It's the perfect excuse to procrastinate. I used to be a soaker too, so I know. I'm not a soaker anymore.

If you're doing your dishes every single day, a pot or a pan will only extremely rarely be truly crusty enough to need soaking. Almost every single time, soaking a dirty cooking pot is an excuse to not actually finish doing the dishes.

If you are convinced a pot has to be soaked, try scrubbing it first. Use a little baking soda if you have to. Pre-scrub before the soak. If you truly can't get the not-yet-dried-up pot clean, go ahead and soak it. But nine times out of ten, you won't

need to, and it will be done. Over. Never to be dealt with again (until the next time you make this soak-worthy dinner).

Running hot water into a soapy pot and leaving it there feels good (and easy) in the moment, but that moment won't last. There's not much grosser than a pot of cold soak-water with bits of last night's dinner floating in it. Nobody wants to stick her hand in that, and it's just too tempting to convince yourself that it probably needs another day of soaking.

And honestly, the most adamant soakers tend to have sinks full of dirty dishes. (Yes, I said it.) So pouring out the dirty soak-water is a gamble. If the dirty water hits a spoon at exactly the right force and angle to send the nasty soak-water right onto the floor, or the counter, or your shirt, that cleanup will be a lot bigger hassle than just washing the pot in the first place.

WIPE IT NOW OR SCRUB IT LATER

Here's a hack that isn't so much a hack as a reality I avoided accepting for way too long.

When something spills, if I deal with it immediately, no matter how large and amazing the splatter pattern, I will get it cleaned in approximately one-tenth the time it would take to clean if I put it off for later.

A broken salsa jar, an overflowing pot of spaghetti sauce, or anything else that makes me lament the universe's vendetta against me is never fun. But wiping up spills immediately, even if I use every clean towel in the house or an entire roll of paper towels, is so much easier and faster than if I stomp out of the kitchen and put off dealing with the mess.

If I wait, either because I "don't have time or energy right now" or because I'm just mad, the job increases exponentially in difficulty. Once it dries, I will have to spray and scrape and scrub.

I'm always tempted to not deal with a mess immediately when it happens because I feel like I haven't had the time to mentally prepare to deal with it. But waiting until later means it's going to be so much more work, so "mentally preparing" will be even more daunting. Meanwhile, I have to live with (or keep everyone out of) a splattered kitchen.

Note: This tip applies anywhere, especially the bathroom. But it's much more pleasant to use salsa and spaghetti sauce as examples instead of, well, y'know.

> When something spills, if I deal with it immediately . . . I will get it cleaned in approximately one-tenth the time it would take to clean if I put it off for later.

PROVIDE A DISH WAND

D ish wands are nothing new, but my mom didn't use one, so they were new to me when my roommate brought one to our college apartment.

Dish wands are the very best way to wash a single dish. Actually, they're the best way to "go ahead and" wash a single dish. Or let me put it this way: dish wands are the best way to eliminate super logical excuses for putting off washing a single dish until there are enough dishes to make washing the dishes worth your time.

Once your dishwashing routine is a mostly daily thing, you'll start to view your dishes differently. Instead of waiting for there to be enough dishes to be "worth your time" to stop whatever else you are doing, you'll have the goal of all your dishes being clean by the end of the day. You'll be working toward your Dishes Finish Line. At that point, one dish is no longer something that should wait until you "do the dishes" but something that can be done quickly to make doing the dishes easier later.

A dish wand makes a single dish doable instead of daunting. There's no need to fill a sink with soapy water. Just use a small amount of water to wet the dish and the dish brush. The soap in the dish brush will let you scrub it out quickly.

I worded the title of this strategy as "provide" a dish wand because it's so much easier to teach other members of your household to deal with single dishes if there's a simple and convenient way to do it.

One last benefit of using a dish wand: You only use just the right amount of dish soap. That's a lot less than a full squirt. Yay for no more soap-flavored chili!

EMPTY THE DISHWASHER

Did you know that emptying your dishwasher is as important as running it? It is, and I'm sorry. I don't like emptying the dishwasher either.

Emptying the dishwasher is one of the easiest household tasks to justify putting off. In the moment, it feels so much easier to grab the dishes you need out of the clean dishwasher to use them. A cup here, a plate there . . . what is the big deal?!

The big deal is that putting off this task halts the routine. If you empty the dishwasher in the morning after running it the night before, then it's available to be filled throughout the day with newly dirtied dishes. This means newly dirtied dishes don't go in the sink. This means that when it's time to run the dishwasher again tonight, all you have to do is gather up any remaining dishes and run it. You don't have to empty what didn't get used throughout the day and then put the dirty dishes from the sink in it.

Empty the dishwasher (or your dish drainer) in the morning if you run your dishwasher in the evening. Your kitchen will look so much better all day.

SAY NO TO KEEP BOXES (OR PILES)

R emember what was missing from the decluttering supplies? I mentioned it in tip 11. A Keep Box. Just say no to Keep Boxes. Keep Boxes are procrastination stations. Almost every graphic you'll ever see for decluttering will include a Keep Box. That drives me bananas. Not having a Keep Box is what makes my decluttering process work. Because Keep Boxes feel so logical, I need to say some more words about why they (and Keep Piles) have to be avoided.

A Keep Box is an excuse to not make a final decision

about something. A Keep Box lets you say you want it, but doesn't make you decide what that means or where it will go, or be realistic about whether you have space for it in your house.

Keep Boxes tend to get shuffled around until they end up in the garage or the attic. In storage. At that point, they're another decluttering project. Skip that step.

You don't need a Keep Box when you use my no-mess decluttering method because you will make a final decision about each item you pull out of a space (one at a time) when you're decluttering. You'll then act on that decision and put the item in the trash or your Donate Box, or you'll take it to its home right then. Doing things this way and not allowing yourself to procrastinate is the key to decluttering for any amount of time and making progress—and only progress.

- *Part 6* -

KITCHEN CLEANING
and
ORGANIZING

MAKE THE MOST OF YOUR DISHWASHER (IF YOU HAVE ONE)

I looooovvvvve my dishwasher so much. But I didn't love it this much until I really understood how to make the most of it. A few simple changes in how I used my dishwasher made a huge impact in how well it cleaned my dishes.

- *Don't be normal.* I used to run every cycle of my dishwasher on the normal setting, no matter what kind of dishes were in it or how dirty they were. Then I visited a lab and met people who design dishwashers. Turns out, those other buttons are there for a *reason*. I still don't analyze each load, but I do use more buttons. I push whatever feels good. I go for turbo or hardcore or megawash or whatever. Normal is for weenies, and simply using more buttons improved the cleanness of my dishes significantly.
- *Use more expensive dishwasher detergent, specifically pods or packets or tabs.* I'm excessively frugal, so I understand if you don't like hearing that. I spent many years confident that more expensive detergent didn't work any better. I was wrong, and my dishes showed it. Here's the basic

rundown of why I was wrong according to what I learned from the scientists in the dishwasher labs. Many detergents had to reformulate when certain ingredients were banned by laws created to protect the environment. This happened at the same time single load packs came on the scene. Single load packs (pods, tabs) quickly became popular (because they're so stinkin' convenient) and got the science when science was needed. If you are convinced your dishwasher is lousy, buy more expensive detergent.

- *Check your dishwasher's mechanics with every load.* Test anything that spins. If a tall cookie sheet or a long spatula blocks the spinner from spinning, the top rack won't get clean. If your dishwasher's detergent door doesn't open, it's likely not the dishwasher's fault. I used to rerun loads several times, and get mad every single time the door didn't open. Turns out, it couldn't open because a cookie sheet was blocking the door!

- *Put heavier items on the bottom rack.* Heavy items on the top rack won't necessarily keep it from cleaning as well, but your racks and sliders will wear out sooner.

- *Point the dirty part of the dish toward the water spray.* Lean plates with their dirty side down. Arrange serving spoons with the soiled side facing the water spray. If you're determined to pack more dishes into the dishwasher, to the point where dishes can't be angled or have the space to get hit by the water, your dishes won't get as clean.

HANDWASH IN THE RIGHT ORDER

If you handwash your dirty dishes, order matters. Just like the way you load a dishwasher matters, the order in which you handwash matters too.

I learned this when I worked in the kitchen at a summer camp. When we stay at my parents' dishwasherless lake house, we have to put it into practice.

Basically, wash your dishes in order of least grody to grodiest.

Wash glasses and cups first. They are filled with liquid, so they (hopefully) don't contain chunks. They're easy to wash and the dishwater will stay clear.

Next come plates that have been scraped off. Use a rubber spatula to scrape plates as clean as a dog would lick them. Or let your dog do it, if that doesn't gross you out. The goal is to remove as much actual food matter as possible before the plates hit the water.

After plates, wash silverware.

After silverware, wash pots and pans (that have been scraped if needed) from least grody to grodiest. Assess grodiness according to greasiness.

You may still need to change out water, but if you follow the grodiness order, you'll need to change the water less often. If you are keeping up and only doing one day's or one meal's worth of dishes at a time, you may not have to change it at all.

CLEAN COUNTERTOPS, STOVETOPS, AND GUNKY DISHES

REMOVE COUNTERTOP STAINS WITH BAKING SODA

I'm not a huge fan of a lot of baking soda cleaning hacks. I don't like the gritty film that's often left behind. I do, however, like using baking soda to clean stains on my laminate kitchen countertops. Double-check your countertop's manufacturer's instructions, but generally it's fine to eliminate stains on laminate and granite counters (though not on natural stone).

Simply sprinkle and scrub with a damp cloth. You'll be amazed.

I once received a cleaning product package for my glass-top stove that included a razor blade. I was scared.

But according to the directions, it wasn't an accident that the razor blade ended up in the box. Once I started using that razor blade to clean my glass cooktop, I was thrilled. Carefully scraping the glass top of my stove (at an angle) was so much more effective, and ridiculously faster, than pouring, spraying, or sprinkling cleaning products on it and scrubbing.

USE AN OLD GIFT CARD TO SCRAPE DISHES

The same concept works on dishes, but for dishes I like to use an old, used-up gift card. That way my kids can use it too, and I don't worry about them damaging the dish or themselves.

When a dish has cooked-on eggs or gravy or anything else, a plastic gift card, minimal dish soap, warm water, and a little elbow grease can easily take care of it. So, you know, *you won't need to soak*.

Note: I prefer to use a plastic gift card over an expired credit card because credit cards tend to have some sort of plastic film covering the front. That plastic film starts to peel after using it for dishes for a while. Most gift cards are one solid piece of plastic so they work better.

COOK (AND CLEAN UP) THE MESSY STUFF IN BATCHES

I f you're an idealist, you may love the idea of cooking from scratch. Cooking from scratch, though, involves the use of pots and pans and causes messes that require cleanup.

I'm putting batch cooking and cleanup under kitchen organizing because organizing is doing something now that will make the future easier. Batch cooking on one day makes cooking dinner on a whole lot of other days so much easier.

I am not a big fan of traditional freezer cooking because I'm not a huge fan of casseroles, and I almost never remember to thaw.

I love cooking several meals' worth of an individual ingredient such as beef, chicken, beans, or rice at one time and then freezing what I don't need for that night's meal. Since I personally cooked the ingredients from scratch, I know how they're made and what is in them, and they make future dinner preps go so much faster and cleanup so much easier.

I generally cook about ten pounds of chicken at once, either under the broiler (a hassle but yummier) or in the slow cooker or Instant Pot (easy and perfectly fine). Then I cool the cooked chicken, freeze it, and use the already cooked chicken in anything that includes a sauce. (Even, sometimes, casseroles.)

I do the same for ground beef. If I brown ten pounds of ground beef at one time, cool it, and then freeze it, I can make tacos or spaghetti or hamburger stew in no time for several weeks.

The biggest perk of batch cooking ingredients this way is that it means minimal cleanup on all those future meals. Dealing with raw chicken and cleaning up the grease that cooks out of hamburger meat is the worst part of cooking. It's not much more work to do it for ten pounds than it is for one pound. Having precooked, mess-free meat saves time and effort in the future and definitely makes it harder to come up with excuses to avoid cooking.

To easily clean up the grease from the ground beef, line the bottom of a large mixing bowl with aluminum foil. Place a colander (preferably one with handles) on the bowl so there is space between the outside-bottom of the colander and the inside-bottom of the bowl. Transfer (one scoop at a time) the browned ground beef from the cooking pan into the colander. Let any grease drip down onto the foil. Once the grease has cooled and hardened, carefully close up the foil over the hardened grease and transfer it to the trash can.

STORE YOUR FOOD CONTAINERS WITH THE LIDS ON

Want to know my number one controversy-sparking tip? Store your food containers with their lids on.

Let's start with why this tip is so controversial. It's the opposite of what the "experts" teach, and it means you can't keep as many.

I match each container to its lid as it comes out of the dishwasher or off of the dish drainer. They get washed at the same time, so they're easy to match up.

This means you don't have to search for a lid that matches the container you already filled with spaghetti sauce while you're in a hurry to get to soccer practice. *That* means you don't have to transfer the spaghetti sauce into a different container when you finally give up on finding the right lid.

When you need to put leftovers away, pull an already-put-together container and matching lid out of your cabinet without having to dig. There's no need to tear apart your carefully (or not) arranged cabinet full of Tupperware. That means you don't cause a crapalanche (a self-explanatory word made up by my friend Cliff Bowen).

But, but, but, you can't fit as many in the cabinet this way! Exactly.

I didn't need as many containers as I was shoving into my cabinet, and that space was a constant disaster because I simply do not naturally take the time to rearrange lids or re-nest bowls after a frantic search for a matching lid. (That's over my Clutter Threshold.)

Not having as many food-storage containers means I run out sooner, and that's a *good* thing. If I run out of containers, I know it's time to clean out the fridge. An unending supply of food containers seems like a good thing, but it isn't. An endless supply means I can keep filling more and more until the ones I filled months ago are shoved in the back of the fridge and the food inside is turning fuzzy.

Fewer containers, stored in a way to make your future easier, is the way to go.

REUSE "GREAT" CONTAINERS RIGHT NOW

'm the daughter of a woman who buys strange food items for the sole reason that she likes the containers they come in. Like pickled mangos. If you love pickled mangos, awesome. But even my mom, who loves everything, didn't necessarily love them. She wanted the jar because it was just so cool.

I get it. I am tempted, every single time I cook with my favorite marinara sauce, to keep the glass jar.

Cool boxes are tough too. It has become a thing for companies to make the act of opening their product's box an "experience." Some of these boxes are *really* good boxes!

My personal rule is that I can keep a box or a glass container if I can use it now. *Right now.* If I can fill the clean

> With this rule, I am not collecting possibilities. I'm using the cool box for a real purpose, and I'm doing it *now*.

spaghetti sauce jar with corn starch and throw away the corn starch box, the jar can stay. If I move my markers into the pretty purple box right this very moment, I can keep the box.

With this rule, I am not collecting possibilities. I'm using the cool box for a real purpose, and I'm doing it *now*. This means I get to feel giddy that I did something great with something cool, or I get a reality check and realize the box doesn't actually make a good pen holder after all. I've learned the hard way that it's better to know whether it works now (*right* now) than to find out after I've stored the box (and six more like it) for a few years.

USE STAIRSTEP PANTRY SHELVING

Kitchens need storage. Canned goods, granola bars, and pasta have to go somewhere! So this is a good time to remind you about the most important quality of storage: get-to-ability. Or findability. Or accessibility.

You need to know what you have (which, for someone like me, means seeing it) and you have to be able to get to it when you need it without rearranging. This is true times ten in the kitchen.

Stairstep shelving in the pantry is so incredibly helpful. Stairstep shelves allow me to be able to see all my canned or jarred goods at one time, without pulling anything out, because they are on levels. I can reach the ones I need, too, without moving anything.

While I absolutely love my expandable stairstep shelves (expandable to match the width of any cabinet), you can make your own stairstep shelves right now.

Grab empty (or mostly empty or could be empty) boxes from your pantry. Empty the ones that aren't. Use hot glue (or regular glue or tape or whatever you have) to attach the boxes together. (Being attached will also make them sturdier.) Ideally (though you should use whatever you have), a Velveeta box makes a good first level and a cracker box makes a good second level. Depending on the size of the cabinet shelf you're using, you could use a cereal box for the third level. If you want to get creative and Mod Podge crafty paper onto your homemade shelf to make it look slightly less homemade, do it now. *Right now.*

Do you see my point that relates to the last tip? Doing this *now* means you don't start collecting empty boxes, thinking you'll build some stairstep shelves later and hoping you'll come up with the very best solution at some point in the future. Doing it now is easy, gets the job done (so you see if you really like doing this), and doesn't provide that beloved excuse for People Like Me to save something just in case.

USE YOUR PANTRY DOOR FOR STORAGE

Here's one of my favorite storage systems, and it's one of the rare times when I will say it might be worth purchasing a system like this. I got mine at The Container Store, but they sell similar systems in many places. I'm a big fan of the ones that don't require tools or drilling to install, so if that's important to you, too, be sure to check.

Adding a back-of-the-pantry-door system was like adding a whole 'nother pantry to my kitchen. It's the perfect size for soup cans and spice packets. There are different-sized "basket racks" to attach so you can make it work for you.

LAZY SUSAN YOUR SPICES

A good collection of spices is essential for any functional kitchen. Like with any kind of storage, get-to-ability is everything with spices. One-handed get-to-ability. I don't carefully read through a recipe and pull out everything I need before I start cooking, so I need one-handed-while-stirring-with-the-other-hand get-to-ability.

I've tried all sorts of methods for storing spices, but fancy methods usually mean taking spices out of their original containers and putting them in matchy-matchy jars that fit in towers or racks. That's over my Clutter Threshold.

Lazy Susans (turntables) are the best solution I've found. With taller spice containers in the middle and shorter ones on the outside edges, I can see all my spices without rearranging anything. I turn until I find what I need, and they're easy to put back.

TURN OLD T-SHIRTS AND CLOTHING INTO CLEANING RAGS

I could have put this tip in several different sections of this book. It could have been a decluttering tip or a closet-decluttering tip. People Who Want to Do the Very Best Thing tend to feel paralyzed over getting rid of stuff that could technically be usable in a desperate situation, but that no one would use unless they were desperate.

Ripped or stained clothing is the perfect example of this dilemma. I won't actually wear a top that's damaged because I have plenty of undamaged options.

But . . . my brain starts wondering if this is the one piece of clothing in the whole wide world that could have saved a random stranger from frostbite, or at least from the shame of public nudity. But then I also imagine the thrift store volunteers who will waste precious time and energy figuring out what to do with this damaged item.

If you're bumfuzzled over why anyone would stress over this stuff, move to the next tip. But this is a legitimate decluttering paralysis factor for People Like Me.

These imagined, plausible dilemmas cause us to just

not do anything. Thinking of all the ways we might do the wrong thing is stressful. Meanwhile, the stress of a messy closet continues.

Cut up your stained, tattered, or ripped T-shirts and use them for rags. If a mess is extra messy or gross, you can throw the rag away.

Here's one more thing (which is more proof that all the concepts in this book have to work together): designate a contained space to store these rags. If your home is overflowing with excess stuff, and this tip makes you feel better about decluttering, you might have so much fun cutting up T-shirts that you end up with bazillions of homemade cleaning cloths. The Container Concept still applies. Once your rag container is full, damaged clothing needs to either go in the trash or be donated to a place that sells damaged clothing for rags.

SCHEDULE YOUR POP-TARTS

Mamas—especially ones on tight budgets—know the frustration of all the favorite food being gobbled up on the first day. I borrowed my best friend, Jennifer's, solution. Schedule your Pop-Tarts. Pop-Tarts are for Sunday mornings when everyone thinks they need a special weekend breakfast, but the morning is hectic as you try to get to church.

Naming Pop-Tarts as your Sunday morning special food means the Pop-Tarts last a whole lot longer than they do when they're a free-for-all.

My husband and I use this concept on our favorite Texas Pecan coffee. It's significantly more expensive than our normal Folgers, so we really can't afford to have it every day. So it's our weekend coffee! Though, honestly, we added Friday morning as the weekend coffee kickoff day a few months ago.

- *Part 7* -

BATHROOM TIPS

and

ORGANIZING

POUR A LITTLE ALL-PURPOSE CLEANER IN THE TOILET-BRUSH HOLDER

P our a small amount of your favorite general-purpose cleaner into your toilet-brush holder. Your bathroom will always smell like it's been recently cleaned, and a quick scrub of your toilet will have more cleaning power than just your own elbow grease.

Don't use hardcore toilet bowl cleaner, since that stuff is scary. It can eat through carpet (I know this for a fact . . .), so it would likely eat through your brush holder.

If you have young kids (or young kids come to your house) ignore this tip. I'm not kidding. You could safely put vinegar in your toilet-brush holder to add oomph to your quick scrubs if you don't mind the smell of vinegar. But don't think your kid would never mess with a toilet brush. Take this advice from the mother of a now-adult kid who thankfully survived chewing on the toilet plunger (and his mother's resulting freak-out) during his potty-training days.

About elbow grease: elbow grease is a euphemism your grandma used for hard work. Don't ask for it in a store. You'll be wasting your time.

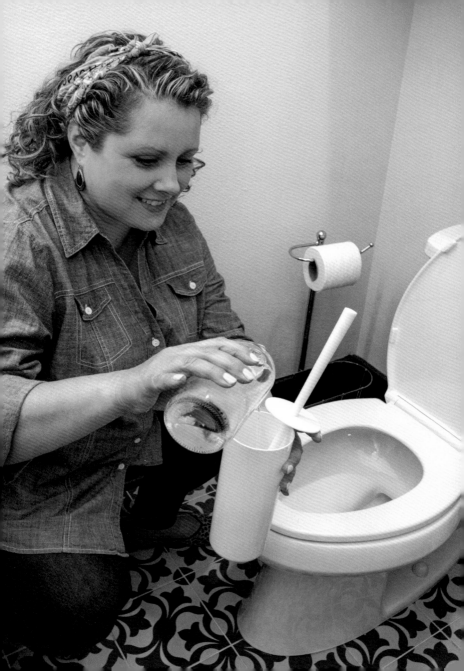

DON'T KNOCK THE QUICK WIPES

Peoule Like Me tend to hear that all the better housekeepers wipe down their bathrooms "quickly" every day. That sounds great, but since we don't trust ourselves (based on lots of experience) to stick with doing it every day, we don't even bother. Or we do it for a few days, see a difference, get excited that we've finally changed, and then realize it has been a month and a half since the last quick wipe and we need to haul out the hazmat suit again.

We like our alls and our nothins. But even if the bathroom is bad (like really, really bad), there's value in the quick wipe. If you've been doing the daily check for clutter (one of the four daily tasks), a quick wipe really is quick. Grab whatever you have (wipes, sprays, rags, or paper towels) and wipe the bathroom counter, the sink, and the toilet (in that order).

If you haven't been checking daily for clutter, straighten a little and wipe what you can, even if it's only getting the toothpaste splatters out of the sink.

Your bathroom will look better. I promise.

And just like with every other cleaning task, this builds. If you wipe the sink today, it will be easier to wipe it again in a few days because the toothpaste buildup will be less than it was today. So maybe you'll wipe the sink and then wipe the counter in the same amount of time it took to do the sink today.

The more often you wipe down your bathroom counter, sink, and/or toilet, the less you'll be in denial about the state of your bathroom and the less time it will take to accomplish an official-in-your-brain bathroom cleaning (because the sink and counter already look pretty good).

UPGRADE YOUR TOILET SEAT

M ost tips in this book don't include buying things. I spent years buying every cleaning gadget I saw, hoping it would solve all my problems. What solved my problems was spending time cleaning my house instead of looking for gadgets that would clean my house.

(If you live in a house with all females, skip this tip. It will be more disturbing than it's worth.)

But if there's a well-spent twenty bucks, it's a new toilet seat with a lid that blocks the wizzle from going into the impossible-to-clean place between the base of the toilet and the tank.

Seriously, y'all. If you have standing urinators in your home, you need a toilet seat with closed hinges. Normal toilet-seat hinges attach to the toilet's base and the toilet's lid with a big gap between them that leaves a clear shot for stray splatters to make their way straight into the impossible-to-clean recesses of the toilet. Closed-hinge toilet seats make a huge difference. There are still splatters, but they can be cleaned. And splatters are more visible so the splatterers can do their own cleaning more easily!

RUN ANYTHING YOU CAN THROUGH THE DISHWASHER

'm a big fan of my dishwasher. If you don't have one, I'm sorry. But all these things can be handwashed too.

In the bathroom, there are actually quite a few things you can wash like you wash dishes. It's a room where a lot of stuff is waterproof anyway (hence fancier-talking countries calling it a "water closet"). Here's a list to look for; just assess your actual items to see if they are dishwasher safe.

- Toothbrushes. Running your toothbrush through the dishwasher, especially on the sanitize cycle, keeps it healthy to use.
- Toothbrush holders. Oh, the splatters. Oh, the grossness inside. Many toothbrush holders are made from glass or plastic that will do great in the dishwasher. If yours is metal, you probably need to handwash it (with dish soap) and dry immediately.
- Soap dishes. Rinse your soap dish and scrape off the big soap bits so you don't end up with a Brady Bunch–style bubble bath in your kitchen.

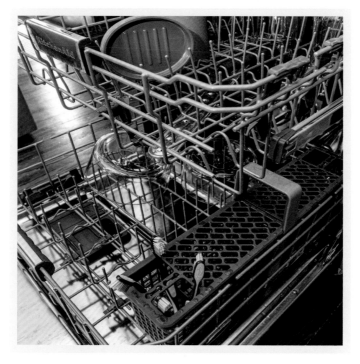

- Pretty containers. Or not-so-pretty ones. If you've put makeup or hair products into a container, it's probably a little gnarly inside.
- Hairbrushes. Not all hairbrushes are dishwasher safe, but many are. If you aren't sure, and you're replacing a hairbrush, put the old one in the dishwasher to experiment.

Things to not put in the dishwasher: anything to do with toilets. Toilets are gross.

CLEAN YOUR STUBBORN GROUT MOLD

I saw this tip on Pinterest and assumed it wouldn't work. Surely it was too simple to clean my grout mold in the awkward spot I could never get clean by scrubbing. But I was desperate, I tried it, and it totally worked.

I put a quarter cup of liquid bleach in a glass jar and dropped six cotton balls into the jar to soak up the bleach. (Adjust for the amount of space you need to clean.) I pulled

the cotton balls out with tongs (while wearing gloves) and lined them up on the moldy grout. I came back an hour later, removed the cotton balls, and the grout looked amazing! Yay!

Only use this trick if you can guarantee your bathroom won't be accessible to children for a few hours. If you live with non-children, you might want to give them a heads-up so they don't pull a Buddy the Elf with the cotton balls on the bathroom floor.

KEEP THESE TWO CLEANING TOOLS IN YOUR SHOWER

A FOOT-SIZED SCRUB BRUSH

As someone who doesn't wake up in the morning excited to clean my shower, I try to make it possible to act on cleaning inspiration in the moment I think of it. When do I think of cleaning the shower? When I'm in it!

Keeping a foot-sized scrub brush in the floor of the shower means I can do a little scrubbing here and there when the thought occurs to me, with my foot, while I condition my hair.

Even without using any cleaning solution, doing this consistently makes a positive impact on the shower. When you do deep clean, the job will be easier and faster to accomplish, and a shower without a grimy floor can go longer between cleanings!

We've already talked about a soap-in-the-handle dish wand in the kitchen section, so this is a good example of the importance of clearly labeling things "for bathroom only."

The beauty of using dish soap to clean the bathroom is that most people feel comfortable with whatever soap they're using to clean their dishes. That means a lot of us are comfortable cleaning the shower with dish soap while we're in it. This means "cleaning the shower" is a whole lot more likely to happen.

Dish soap (clearly labeled for the bathroom) and a non-scratch scrubby sponge work wonders, but an even quicker and easier way to do a little scrubbing here and there while you're in the shower is to keep a dish wand with soap in the handle hanging in the shower. That way, as you shower, and you happen to see a spot that needs to be scrubbed, you can go ahead and scrub it between rinsing your right and left armpits.

REMOVE (OR PREVENT) SOAP SCUM

If you have a glass shower door, you might hate it—especially if you live in an area with hard water. I understand why fancy-schmancy showers are designed without a door at all. My house, unfortunately, isn't fancy-schmancy.

Ideally, use a squeegee. Consistent squeegeeing (like, every single time) will eliminate the need for much more than a shine when you "officially" clean your shower. It will also make you feel less guilty about going a lot longer between shower cleanings.

The best way to get family to cooperate with every-single-time squeegeeing is repeated lengthy lectures and awkward entire-family-standing-in-the-bathroom moments where the one who cares demonstrates (fully clothed) how easy the process is. Eventually (hopefully), they will start squeegeeing to avoid the awkwardness.

Or, there's Rain-X (or similar water-repelling products). Rain-X on car windshields works like magic, sending water flying off the windshield. Rain-X makes a product specifically for shower doors that repels water, not giving anything a chance to cause buildup. Follow Rain-X's directions carefully to stay safe. You do not want something slick (that *stays* slick) dripping on your bathroom floor.

Squeegees and Rain-X prevent soap-scum buildup, but I wouldn't be me if I didn't address what's bouncing around in the brains of My People: "What do you do when there's *already* a *lot* of hard water/soap scum/whatever-that-white-stuff-is built up?" Good old dish soap and scrubby sponges (get the non-scratch kind) will make a big difference, but I like to do that *after* I pull out my credit card. My old and expired credit card. Or a used-up gift card. Use the edge of the card to scrape off the soap scum. A razor would work too, but a plastic gift card or credit card makes this a great job for a kid.

If you use a shower curtain instead of a glass door, the best way to clean the liner is to . . . not. You can have a new shower curtain liner delivered to your home every month (or every other month) with a subscription on Amazon. That's what I do. I used to try to wash them and scrub them, and I stressed about whether it was safe to put them in the washing machine (it's generally not, especially modern machines), and then a friend whose house is always clean acted like I was crazy. She just replaces them regularly. I took that as permission that I could do that too.

Bonus tip: When you wash a fabric shower curtain in the washing machine, don't stress out about where to hang it up to dry. The perfect place to hang your shower curtain to dry is . . . on the shower curtain rod. In the bathroom. Where it goes anyway.

LABEL YOUR BATHROOM CLEANING STUFF

Since we're talking about cleaning the bathroom, let's talk about how cleaning the bathroom is gross. That can be a real hang-up for a lot of people. The thought of touching nasty things that have touched nasty things (even your own nasty things) can be paralyzing. But the longer you put off cleaning, especially in gross spaces, the grosser those spaces become, which makes cleaning that space even more daunting.

The next few bathroom tips are specifically designed to prevent cleaning paralysis. If grossness paralyzes you, questioning whether you used a particular sponge or scrub brush in the bathroom or the kitchen will paralyze you more. And then there's the heart stoppage that happens when you see your kid cleaning (yay!) but you don't know for sure where she found the sponge she's using (yikes!).

Label your bathroom cleaning stuff (like the dish wand in your shower). Don't pull out the (or buy a) label maker. Grab a permanent marker. Black is best, but use hot pink if that's all you have. Write "Bathroom ONLY" right on the scrubber or the cloth or the sponge itself. This little trick will prevent cross-contamination, help you sleep better, and/ or let you know how hard to freak out if you see your kid wiping down the kitchen table.

LABEL YOUR REUSABLE CLEANING CLOTHS BY SURFACE

Have you figured out that a lot of my advice (based on what I've had to do in my own home for my own brain) basically boils down to "do what ya gotta do"? I have no problem using disposable wipes or paper towels. They make cleaning easy. When cleaning is easy, it's more likely to happen.

If you don't want to use disposable products, great, *as long as you go ahead and clean.* This sounds like advice that shouldn't need to be dished out, but my role as a Cleaning Expert has proven that even the obvious needs to be stated.

The appeal of disposable products for someone like me (who suffers from undiagnosed-so-possibly-not-official-but-still-occasionally-debilitating germaphobia) is that once a disposable wipe is gross, I can throw it away and never touch it again. But if you suffer from real or imagined germaphobia *and* you can't bring yourself to use trashable products *or* trust yourself to remember exactly which rag has touched what and where, label your cleaning cloths with the permanent marker. Or color code or embroider them. Do whatever you have to do (that you can do today) to help you feel confident so cleaning actually happens.

CREATE YOUR OWN HAZMAT SUIT

'm not a psychologist and I don't know the diagnostic criteria for a germaphobe. Also, we're not talking about an actual hazmat suit that would work in an actual hazmat situation. Now that I have those caveats out of the way, I'll call myself an unofficial, undiagnosed germaphobe. The fact that I'm unable to use a fork that touched a restaurant table means friends are usually surprised to learn that cleaning is a big-time struggle for me.

The truth is, being freaked out by germs makes it hard to clean gross stuff. The longer gross stuff goes without being cleaned, the grosser it gets, and the more freaked out I get. Mental gymnastics and animated conversations with myself help, but garbing up helps most. Gloves. Get a good pair to help you be willing to scrub what needs scrubbing. I hang my reusable cleaning gloves on a hook under my bathroom counter. If you can't make yourself reuse gloves, packages of medical gloves are inexpensive and can be ordered online.

Always ventilate areas where you're using cleaning products, but if you still worry about what you're breathing, wear a mask. *Most of us have those now.*

Cover your hair with a bandana, scarf, or Buff if you worry about scratching your head while chemicals are on your (gloved) hand. Choose your "cleaning outfit." It can be shorts and a T-shirt or turtleneck, sweatpants, and galoshes. If you worry about washing your cleaning clothes with other clothes, wash them on their own. Or declutter your closet, label a box of clothes you hate "Bathroom Cleaning Clothes," and throw them away every time.

This tip is getting more ridiculous. I'm freaked out by grody stuff, so I put off doing grody stuff. Meanwhile, stuff gets grodier, which freaks me out more. I have to break the cycle. If I need a ridiculous, homemade hazmat(ish) suit to be willing to clean, great. Do whatever you have to do.

Here's good news: Every time you gear up and get to work, your bathroom will look better, and you'll feel less overwhelmed next time. The more you do what it takes to get over your hang-ups, the fewer hang-ups you'll have. The toilet won't be as gross. The grime around the faucets will be a little less grimy. Maybe you'll be able to throw your cleaning clothes in the washer next time or reuse the gloves. You'll probably be able to use milder products. Or maybe not. Whatever it takes is whatever it takes.

Oh, and also—knee-pads. Not that they help with germaphobia, but they definitely help with excuse-busting. I'm a lot more likely to do hands-and-knees cleaning when I know I'll still be able to walk after I'm done.

MAKE IT AS EASY AS POSSIBLE TO REPLACE THE TOILET PAPER ROLL

We used to use traditional screwed-to-the-wall toilet paper holders, but I've found these inexpensive toilet paper holder/storage combos to be much better in our home. "Installing" a new roll of toilet paper is simply a matter of sliding the roll onto the bar. There are no extra steps or the need to hold the roll just so while squeezing the bar and getting it into the holder before you release. I mean, sometimes that feels like a hassle. The lack of extra steps involved in installing a new toilet paper roll significantly decreases the temptation to "save time" by standing a new roll vertically on top of the empty roll.

Extra toilet paper rolls are stored right in the holder, and I especially like this toilet paper holder that includes a magazine rack that's perfect for storing feminine products. If you want to keep the package discreet, most will fit easily into a soft-sided makeup bag.

STORE YOUR EXTRAS IN THE PLACE WHERE YOU NEED THEM

The convenience of getting to something the moment I actually need it has to be the deciding factor in where to store it.

But I have to achieve balance in how much I can think about these decisions, especially in the bathroom. I need to store bathroom stuff in the bathroom. It's the room in the house where I am when I need things most desperately and immediately and in the most inconvenient state of dress or undress.

There may be more storage space in your basement, or even in the storage closet by the back door of the house, but nobody wants you running naked through the house in a desperate search.

But where things go within the bathroom has to be determined by that first decluttering question: *Where would I look for it first?* Even if it feels logical to store hand soap refills in the cabinet under the sink, if you look for hand soap refills in the cabinet over the toilet, you could end up buying more hand soap refills even though there's a year's worth "hidden" directly under the place where you washed your hands with shampoo last week. I know this to be fact.

Embrace the place where you'd look first as any item's true home, and accept the realities of the space you have. If you don't have much storage space in the bathroom, you don't have much storage space in the bathroom. That's the Container Concept. Let your limits force you to identify what really needs to be in that space and give you the freedom to let other things go.

Organize according to the way you actually live. Put things in the places you'll be when you're desperate for them and in the spot you actually look for them. See how that improves your everyday life.

> Embrace the place where you'd look first as any item's true home, and accept the realities of the space you have.

FOLLOW THESE TOWEL TIPS

HOOK UP YOUR TOWELS

Towels on the bathroom floor can make mama minds feel like they're going to explode. Or spouse minds, or roommate minds.

Towel hooks (which are installed by simply hanging them over the door, no tools needed) placed as near as possible to the place where the towel drops anyway, are a great solution. Towels that are hung to dry can be reused for several showers or baths. That means there are fewer towels to wash on Laundry Day!

Just remember that hanging a towel instead of letting it drop to the floor is a habit to be developed. The daily clutter check in the bathroom will help develop this habit.

ROLL, DON'T FOLD

I am the world's worst folder. It's not that I've tried and failed, it's that I don't actually care. I don't mind folding towels, though. Towels need to be stored in a way that allows one to be removed without the entire stack becoming a jumbled mess.

Technically, I don't fold towels; I roll them. Rolling towels is less precise, so kids can do it as well as I can. Depending on the size of the towel, I fold it over in the middle, then fold two to three times lengthwise, and then roll. Rolled towels stay rolled while I carry them to the cabinet where they are stored, vertically, in a basket inside the cabinet. Pulling out one towel doesn't (usually) send the entire stack tumbling.

Strategy 75

CONTAIN YOUR HAIR AND BEAUTY SUPPLIES

T he older I get, the more desperation purchases I make in the beauty department. The natural look is less appealing on me than it used to be. This means I try more hair and skincare products, and without a limit, the ones that aren't being used tend to stick around.

My friend Lea (who is amazing at home management stuff) advised me long ago to put the stuff that stays out on my bathroom counter in a clear plastic shoebox. She does that so she can easily move the shoebox (instead of individual products) to clean the bathroom counter.

The bonus perk (that Lea didn't need) is that the plastic shoebox serves as a limit for my products. The size of the shoebox determines how many products I can or should keep so they don't take over the bathroom counter. When the shoebox is full, and I bring in a new face serum that's full of hope, something has to go to make room because the size of the shoebox is the limit to how many products I can keep at one time.

Part 8

LIVING AREAS

PRIORITIZE SPACE FOR LIVING

My number one strategy for living areas is to give priority to empty space. If you happen to be one of My People, you may not have thought much about why you call your living room your *living* room. We do a lot of living in our living room. That's where we binge *Seinfeld*, have tough conversations, and repeatedly throw the dog's favorite toy. Our living room is where we live life together as a family and where we chat with people who come into our home. We bought our house to live in it. We didn't sign a mortgage so we could have a storage space for random stuff, but so we could have a place to build relationships.

As I decluttered (randomly at first), I learned to place more value on space than on stuff. Having less stuff in my home meant it was easier to move around, easier to do the things I needed (or wanted) to do.

> **Just because a space is empty doesn't mean it is available to fill with stuff.**

Pay attention to space. If this is the room where you want to lounge with your family, there needs to be seating that isn't easily taken over by piles of stuff. There should be open space for bringing in a few extra chairs if you have a party. If there's an ottoman, it needs to be available to put your feet up after a long day, instead of piled with stuff.

Living requires open space for your body and your family's bodies. Just because a space is empty doesn't mean it is available to fill with stuff. It's empty for a reason, and that reason is that someone may need, at any given moment, to plop down there in exhaustion, excitement, or despair.

Work toward making living spaces under-full so there's space for the intangible.

EMBRACE THE E-READER

Are you ready for what could be the most controversial, panty-wadding tip in this book? Here you go: get an e-reader.

I know you like books. I'm glad you like books. I'm counting on this one to pay for a semester or so of college for one of my kids. I also love books, and I love to read on my e-reader. I resisted it too, though, so let me clear up some common misunderstandings. I'm not talking about reading books on an app on your smartphone or a tablet you can also use to check email. I'm talking about an actual e-reader that is only used for reading books.

I understand you like to smell the book and turn the pages. I do too, and I have lots of books in my home that I love. *But I also have an e-reader* and that little device keeps me from having shelves (or honestly, the floor next to my bed) piled with books I don't actually love.

If I love a book, I buy it in physical form. A physical book has to earn shelf space on my decluttered shelves.

Here's what I love about my e-reader. An actual e-reader (as opposed to a smartphone or tablet) doesn't have the blue light screen. It looks eerily like paper. An e-reader connects to Wi-Fi to download books, but doesn't have an internet browser. I can't use it to check my email. *I don't want to check my email.* I want a book to be an escape.

Now for the stuff that makes me like an e-reader *better* than a traditional book. An e-reader is lightweight no matter how long the book I'm reading. I can lean it against something, and it doesn't flop closed. If I'm reading in bed (like I do every night), I don't have to flip from side to side if I'm at a point in the book when it's significantly heavier on one side than the other. I lean the e-reader against my husband's arm, or prop it on my nightstand, and all I have to do to turn a page is poke one finger out from my blanket cocoon to tap the page. When I fall asleep, it turns off.

I can read a book in the bathtub without fretting about getting it wet because I stick my e-reader in a Ziploc bag.

I can change the font size, a necessity now that I'm pushing fifty.

And last but *definitely* not least, library books return themselves. I had stopped using my local library because I *always* ended up with late fees. (Or replacement fees . . .) I can check out an e-book without leaving my house. And when time is up, it disappears! (Frustrating if I'm not finished, but not as frustrating as double-digit late fees.)

With an e-reader, I have endless reading material that I can stick in my purse or my suitcase, and not fill up my bookshelves.

DECORATE WALLS OVER SURFACES

I f you struggle with clutter, focus your decorating efforts on adorning walls instead of surfaces. This tip is for People Like Me who have lower-than-we-wish Clutter Thresholds.

I love a beautiful tableau of knickknacks in someone else's home, but I've learned those tableaus are above my Clutter Threshold. A display of candlesticks and vases and plaques with cutesy sayings will get knocked over by my dog or my kid and I won't even notice until other random not-decorative things like mail and batteries and lightbulbs have joined the pile.

If I focus on decorating walls, the work I do doesn't depend on tweaking, rearranging, or maintaining. At least, not as much.

AVOID LONG-TERM STORAGE IN THE LIVING ROOM

U ltimately, this is a mindset shift that goes along with prioritizing living in the living room. The fact that you should not use your living room as a storage area feels obvious when you read it, but it's not uncommon for those who "don't have room for all our stuff" to stack boxes or fill bins full of craft supplies on your living room bookshelves.

As you declutter your living room (soon, if you're following the Visibility Rule), make it your goal to eliminate storage from this space. Family games you'll play in this room placed in a small cabinet that doubles as an end table are fine. Family games stored in tubs that are stacked in the corner? Not so much. Tubs of outgrown clothes that you're keeping in case your cousin has a baby? Definitely not.

PURGE BIG STUFF

et's talk about the value and impact of purging big stuff—furniture, decorative giraffes, stuff like that. We're dealing with living rooms specifically in this section, but this tip applies everywhere in your home.

Identify furniture pieces you despise, and get them out of your house. If you think you love all your furniture, pay attention to anything that makes the path through your living room hard to walk. Notice tables you're always bumping into and chairs no one likes because they're lumpy.

I know this sounds too simple. Furniture is supposed to be useful, so it's a natural decluttering hang-up to think you should keep it. It also feels right to keep big stuff because of the expense required to replace it. Even if you only spent fifteen bucks at a garage sale, the regret of paying retail if you end up wishing you'd kept it makes your heart palpitate.

But eliminating large pieces of furniture opens up large amounts of space instantly. This can be a big leap down the path to changing your home. I'm not saying to get rid of your favorite recliner. I'm saying to get rid of the stuff you don't like, but for whatever reason thought you couldn't get rid of.

If you wish your house were bigger, get rid of something big. Empty floor space and walls with nothing shoved against them make your house feel better and bigger. Removing an average desk from a room opens up fifteen square feet of floor space. An average living area (according to geteasymove.com) is 330 square feet. A room that size becomes 4.5 percent larger by removing a desk.

My living room is approximately 300 square feet. For years, I moved a very large chair and its matching ottoman around and around and around. The chair blocked doorways, was regularly piled with clean clothes (before I started folding straight out of the dryer), and was generally a problem. But the chair matched my couch, and it was the first set of real furniture I'd ever purchased as a grownup.

Every time I stuff-shifted that chair out of a room, I liked the room it left more. That room grew by twelve square feet. But the room I shifted it to shrank twelve square feet. Once I got that chair out of my house, my house grew.

Big thing gone. Big weight lifted from my brain. Big space opened up.

ELIMINATE FLAT SURFACES (AT LEAST SOME OF THEM)

No flat surface is safe in my home. I can create a pile of random stuff with zero awareness I'm doing it. Things leave my hands without any notice of when or where they left.

This is similar to the "remove big stuff" tip, but can offer additional perks. I've learned that if a desk or table or shelf refuses to stay clutter-free, if it continually morphs back into disaster, I need to consider eliminating the surface. If there is no chair to pile with coats, I end up (usually) putting them where they actually go. If there isn't a super-convenient surface to drop mail onto as I come into the house, I am more likely to head straight to the trash can to throw away 90 percent of it.

> **No flat surface is safe in my home. I can create a pile of random stuff with zero awareness I'm doing it.**

Strategy 82

FIGHT PET HAIR

I have a German shepherd. If you have one too, you know that statement is all the credential I need to speak on the subject of dealing with dog hair. I wouldn't trade my big, crazy baby for anything in the world, but oh my word, the amount of hair she sheds is shocking.

Not only is the hair on the floors, it's on the couches. Dog hair officially gets everywhere in our living spaces. Here are my best tips for dealing with dog hair.

When you find a tool you like, keep multiples of it in various, easily accessible areas of the house, wherever you're going to need it. Like Dishes Math, Dog Hair Math is a thing, so dealing with small amounts immediately is easier than letting it build.

A good vacuum that can easily transition between carpet and hard floors is incredibly helpful, but for a quick cleanup, I like to keep a floor duster easily accessible to quickly deal with the edges of the room. All floor dirt and debris, especially dog hair, gravitates to the edges of the room.

A few times a year, I purchase a five-pack of tape rollers at Costco, since that's what my family will use most frequently, and they like to have them available to get dog hair off of their clothes. But tape rollers can run out, especially if I'm using them all the time. For this reason, I love the reusable ChomChom Roller. It picks up hair on furniture well, though it kind of grosses me out to empty it. One last trick is to put on a rubber glove and run your hand along the furniture. This does a great job getting up the hair, though it is a bit of a pain to clean it off.

CLEAN THE CEILING FAN WITHOUT COVERING YOUR HAIR IN DUST

As a woman in her later forties, I can't live without my ceiling fan. I could not care less if ceiling fans are a design faux pas. Mama needs a breeze blowing on her at all times. Nobody's happy when mama is hot.

Y'all, if you want proof that there's dirt and dust in the air in your home, look at a ceiling fan that hasn't been dusted in a while. It's shocking what will collect on the blades. The best cleaning option is to gently dust the blades as part of a regular routine so it never builds to a clumpy, scary mess.

But if that hasn't happened, or if you never see the dust clumps because your ceiling fan is always on, here's the best solution I've found (out of the many solutions I've tried).

Turn off the fan. (I feel like that's obvious, but just in case . . .) While on a sturdy ladder or stepstool (you don't want to grab the ceiling fan for balance), carefully slide a pillowcase over one fan blade at a time, not putting any weight or pressure on the blade itself to avoid messing up the fan's balance. Gently slide the pillowcase off the blade using the

pillowcase to grab the majority of the dust buildup. If any dust is left, you can use a soft duster to remove it.

It's important to note that my number one reason/excuse for avoiding cleaning ceiling fans was that I didn't want dust clumps falling on my hair or into my eyeballs. Avoiding dusting my ceiling fans, though, (obviously) just meant fan blades got clumpier. Using the pillowcase as a duster allows me to catch the dust without causing a huge mess. Flip the pillowcase inside out and shake it into the trash can or outside, and throw the pillowcase into the laundry hamper.

- *Part 9* -

CLOTHING

and

LAUNDRY TIPS

START WITH THE STUFF IN THE BOTTOM OF THE DRAWER

As we start talking about decluttering and organizing tips for stuff you wear, I think it's important to acknowledge that People Like Me can have a hard time accepting that clothing can be clutter. Before I started my deslobification process, I'd honestly never considered this, but it was my overabundance of clothing that helped me come up with my definition of clutter: anything that consistently gets out of control in my home. Clothing definitely got out of control. Very consistently.

Finding a laundry routine that worked for me did more than anything else to help me identify which clothes should go, and it helped me be willing to let them go. If all your clothes are consistently clean, you'll have all of them to choose from each week. You'll see which ones don't get picked when there are other clean options, .

These are the clothes at the bottom of the drawer. While you put clean clothes away, you'll see which clothes haven't been worn in a while. Those should be easy to declutter, especially if the drawer doesn't close while you're putting away the clothes you did wear. Just remember, the drawer is a container, so it's the natural limit to how many clothes you can keep.

Strategy 85

USE HOOKS

JEWELRY STORAGE

'm not a fashionista by any means, but I do like my costume jewelry. Storing my necklaces was a disaster for years, and I ended up throwing away tangles of necklaces at least once a year. I tried jewelry stands and hanging organizers, but those proved to be above my Clutter Threshold when they knocked over or fell off the wall.

What finally worked was a tip sent to me by a blog reader. She sent me a picture of her jewelry hanging on hooks screwed straight into her wall. It made sense to me and I tried it. It isn't the mostest beautifulest solution, but it works better than any of the other solutions I've tried. I hang both earrings and necklaces on the hooks right next to my bathroom mirror, and the solution has worked well for me for years. If you don't like the idea of putting holes in your walls, removable Command hooks would work too.

Ultimately, like any successful organizing solution, the hooks are a container. I can't keep screwing more hooks into my wall until the entire bathroom is covered. There is a limit to how many hooks can go in the space I have to devote to this solution, and then there's a limit to how many necklaces I can store on each hook and still be able to remove them easily. When the hooks are full, I know it is time to declutter jewelry. Usually, that's easy.

CAPS AND HATS

We also use hooks to store caps. I have two sons, and they have a lot of baseball caps. Baseball caps are great souvenirs, they get passed out at special events, and friends and relatives give them as gifts. I got so tired of finding "special" caps crumpled at the bottom of a pile, and I got tired of feeling irritated when one of them needed a cap but couldn't find even one of the many I knew they had.

When they hang their caps on hooks, the hats can be displayed and cherished, but they're also easily accessible to be worn. And of course, there are a limited number of hooks, so they serve as a natural container.

KEEP A DONATE BOX
NEXT TO THE DRYER

L ooking at a mass of clothing, either in piles or stacks, or even in your closet or drawers, is overwhelming, and decluttering the mass is often a daunting process.

While that daunting process is necessary, one easy way to continually declutter clothes is to keep a Donate Box (a donatable one, of course) right by your dryer. When you pull things out of the dryer, especially if you are folding them immediately, you're touching and seeing individual items. You'll often realize something is outgrown or damaged or out of style during this process.

Having a Donate Box right in the spot where this process happens weekly means you can act on these instincts immediately and declutter clothing as you go.

DON'T LET IMPERFECT CLOTHES BE YOUR PARALYSIS POINT

Decluttering Paralysis can flare up when you run across imperfect clothing because you're just not sure what to do with something that may be damaged, but could technically still be worn if someone was desperate for something to wear.

Call the place where you donate clothes and ask if they want imperfect clothing. I hate making phone calls too, but this quick phone call will give you so much freedom in all your future clothing decluttering projects. I say to ask because many places sell torn and stained (clean, but stained) clothing to rag makers, and they will tell you to pretty please donate your imperfect clothing. This knowledge will help you get rid of more clothing, more quickly.

If the place where you donate clothing doesn't want imperfect clothes, you'll be free to throw them away because you'll know. When I declutter clothing, I like to have an extra Donate Box or bag handy for the imperfect clothing. I label it "Imperfect." This makes me feel better, but honestly, the donation centers I've asked have said this isn't necessary.

Strategy 87

EMBRACE THE MAGIC OF HANGERS

GET THE GOOD HANGERS

One of the best inventions for keeping my own closet neat(er) than it would otherwise be is the velvet hanger. Velvet hangers are generally available anywhere hangers are sold. I love velvet hangers because any clothing, even slippery blouses or tank tops, fits well on the hanger and stays in place even if it would slide right off of a plastic hanger. I have a hard enough time keeping things neat, so I definitely don't need clothes falling off hangers onto the floor!

DECIDE WHAT IS HANGER-WORTHY

Let your good hangers help you declutter clothes. I love velvet hangers, but they aren't cheap (which is why my kids don't get them). This means I don't want to keep buying more every time I use up a box. But that's a good thing. A limited number of velvet hangers is (you know what I'm about to say) a container. It's a limit.

If you decide to purchase velvet hangers, switch them out for your old hangers purposefully. Choose your favorite

clothing items first to put on your new velvet hangers. Once the limited number of hangers has been used, declutter all (or at least a lot of) the clothes that weren't hanger-worthy.

This works for ongoing clothing decluttering as well. If I pull an item of clothing out of the dryer (so I know I like it because I just wore it), but there are no velvet hangers available to put it on, I ask myself which velvet-hung piece of clothing is less hanger-worthy than the one I just pulled out of the dryer. I stick that piece in the handy-dandy Donate Box that is right by the dryer.

DESIGNATE A HOOK RACK FOR NOT-DIRTY-BUT-NOT-CLEAN CLOTHES

I had to eliminate the chair where I piled clothes I'd worn once, but that could be worn again. Even though I placed clothes there with the good intentions of wearing them again, it quickly turned into a pile where clothes were lost.

I designated an over-the-door multi-hook rack for these clothes instead. The hooks are perfect for hanging and airing out clothes I want to wear again.

And of course, best of all, the hook rack is a container. Once the hooks are full, it's time to act. Clothes either need to go into the laundry or my closet. They can't keep piling like they did on the chair.

It's important to also note that putting worn-but-not-dirty clothes back in the closet is a perfectly valid option. I mean, if they're clean enough to wear again, then they're clean enough to be put away.

But if you *just can't*, like I *just can't*, the hooks work.

Strategy 89

CONSOLIDATE

Part of the final step of my decluttering process is to consolidate. Put like things together. This is key for clothing, and is an easy and somewhat enjoyable process in the closet. If your closet is packed full, take a moment to consolidate. Move things around (without pulling everything out), and put dresses together, pants (or, if you're British, trousers) together, blouses together.

Then consolidate further by putting short-sleeved blouses together, and then further by putting black short-sleeved blouses together, and so forth.

Consolidating does two things. It makes you notice individual items instead of just seeing an overwhelming category of "clothing." That alone will generally reveal quite a few *duh* items that can go into the Donate Box.

Consolidating also reveals that you may have doubles or octupoles of certain things like black short-sleeved blouses. Seeing them together may reveal that some are faded or wonky or just don't fit correctly and that you'll be fine if they're gone since you have plenty.

HANG WITH PURPOSE

I hang as many clothes as I possibly can. First of all, they are (more) likely to stay wrinkle-free this way. Drawers are for clothes that I don't mind getting wrinkled.

This worked especially well for my kids. When my kids were little, I was convinced they had been born completely without fashion sense, without the awareness of which clothes could be worn together. Hanging helped.

Anything that was to be worn to school (they have a dress code at their public school, so there's a definite difference between school clothes and regular clothes) went on a hanger in the closet. Anything for other times went in drawers. This simple distinction kept my kids on track.

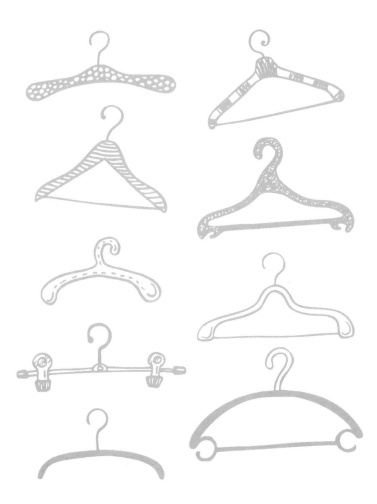

USE COLORED HANGERS TO KEEP FAMILY LAUNDRY SORTED

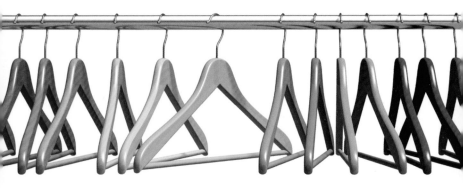

When kids are young, a two-year age difference may make it pretty obvious whose clothes are whose. Once puberty hits, anyone in the family can be any size. Or the same size.

My kids' school dress code meant the T-shirts they could wear to school were all the same four colors. I tried all sorts of systems for keeping their clothes straight. I hung clothes on three different doorknobs (both sides of the laundry room door and a nearby closet) as I pulled them out of the dryer.

That kind of worked, but I often forgot whose doorknob was whose, had to double-check, and regularly got mixed up. Then I had to remember whose clothes were in which hand as I put them into the closets. Then, my kids had to remember which side of the shared closet was whose (even though they'd used the same side their entire life, but whatever) and no one touched the clothes in the middle because they weren't sure where one person's wardrobe ended and another's began.

It shouldn't have been complicated, but it totally was. I blame all the remembering and double-checking that was required.

As I shopped one August while every display held college dorm supplies, it hit me. Different-colored hangers. It's so *duh*, but it changed everything. I assigned one color to each kid, and now I don't have to sort onto different doorknobs. I only check sizes one time. Everyone knows their color, so they don't have to ask or double-check either.

THE SOCK BASKET OR THE LAUNDRY BAG

My friend Connie has eight kids, and she's funny. When people ask how she manages her large family, she responds, "Oh, it's easy. I just don't fold underwear."

I've never even thought about folding underwear, but for years, I matched socks and put them in drawers.

Now we have a sock basket. I ordered a basket-like plastic tub that fits right under the dryer door. As socks come out, I drop them in the basket. I realized I was spending a lot of my fold-right-out-of-the-dryer time matching socks, and sometimes two socks from one pair ended up in different loads. Dumping all the socks into the sock basket makes folding time go faster, and everyone knows where to look for clean socks.

The sock basket isn't universally loved by everyone in the family, so I give the persnickety ones another option. When someone complains, I offer him/her (but really, him) a small, washable laundry bag to keep his/her (but really, his) socks together. That puts the work on the person who cares. If someone doesn't want his/her (but really, his) socks mixed with other people's socks, he can use a laundry bag. Oops. I meant he/she.

Complaints had happened before the sock basket. Laundry bags had been purchased and offered. But it wasn't until the sock basket system was implemented (and the Mom-matches-and-distributes-socks-to-drawers system was discontinued) that the beauty of the laundry bag and the need for personal responsibility was accepted. Laundry bags are available to all. You can implement your own system, or you can live with Mom's. It's your choice.

USE LAUNDRY TONGS

L aundry tongs are my favorite laundry tool. They eliminate some of my best excuses for putting off doing laundry.

This was a suggestion a blog reader made when I lamented that my new washing machine was so big (yay!) that I couldn't reach that last sock in the bottom of it (boo!). Technically I could reach it, but I had to stand on a stool

and felt like I was going to topple headfirst into the washing machine.

I now use a pair of tongs that have lost the attachment to make them stay closed. That made them unfun to cook with, but perfect for grabbing socks out of the why-is-it-so-deep washing machine and the why-does-it-go-so-far-back dryer. The tongs I use have a smooth edge so they won't snag clothing. I hang my tongs on a hook right by the dryer.

Pro tip: Don't get mad if someone in your house puts your laundry tongs in the dishwasher because they don't know laundry tongs are a thing. They're trying to be helpful. Just explain they're laundry tongs now. Keep smiling when they look at you like you're crazy.

Strategy 94

USE FEWER LAUNDRY BASKETS

How many laundry baskets do you need? If you're asking that question, my answer is, "Fewer than you have." I have one, and most weeks I don't use it.

Once upon a time, when my laundry was totally out of control, I had at least seven laundry baskets, including a super-fancy set that stacked up to create a laundry sorting system.

If you have laundry under control, you can ignore this tip. If you and your family can count on finding clean drawers (Southern slang for undies) every time you open your actual drawers, you're good. Keep doing what you're doing, even if it's a system that depends on seven laundry baskets.

But if you live in constant, substantiated fear of an empty drawers drawer, you do not need more laundry baskets. I once also believed that not having enough laundry baskets (or the right-shape or right-size laundry baskets) was the reason I didn't have laundry under control. I thought buying more laundry baskets would help, so I bought more. When that didn't help, I bought even more. Different ones, but more. And I didn't get rid of the old ones.

I have decluttered many (*maaaaannnnnyyyyy*) laundry baskets during my deslobification process. Laundry baskets don't help get laundry under control. Laundry that's under control is laundry that's being washed, dried, and put away routinely. Consistently.

It's all about the routine, and if the routine includes putting clean clothes away, there really isn't a time when clean laundry needs to sit in baskets.

Let me clarify that laundry baskets and laundry hampers aren't the same thing. We have a laundry hamper for each bedroom. That's where dirty clothes go. I like the rolling ones that make it easy to take them to the laundry room.

Laundry baskets for clean clothes are procrastination stations. Try decluttering laundry baskets as you work on creating your laundry routine. Not having procrastination stations available will force you to complete the routine. Once you do that, you'll see that you can let the laundry baskets go.

FOLD CLOTHES STRAIGHT
OUT OF THE DRYER

We've talked about procrastination stations. A recliner (dresser, loveseat, dining table, pool table) piled with laundry is the ultimate procrastination station. And unfolded/ wadded laundry is the ultimate eyesore procrasticlutter. No matter how hard you work to "pick up" or "clean" or even "declutter" a room, if there's a teetering pile of clothes on any surface, the space will not look clean. Five loads of laundry piled on five different surfaces make the whole house look insane. I know this for a fact and from experience.

I also know from personal experience that if you don't fold straight out of the dryer, you have super logical excuses for why you don't. My excuses were amazing too, but I was wrong. (And so are you.)

I said I could fold laundry anywhere. That's true. I said I could fold while I watched TV. True. I said I could get the next load from the washer to the dryer sooner if I dumped the dryer's load in a laundry basket. That's technically, mostly true. I said I could dump it on my bed, and *have* to fold it before I went to bed that night. That one wasn't the least bit true.

The problem with these reasons for not folding straight out of the dryer is the word *could*. *Could* means something might happen. It's possible. But when the thing that could happen never happens, your *could* is an excuse.

What *actually* happens matters more than what *could* happen. In reality, I took clean laundry somewhere, went back to put wet clothes into the dryer, and completely forgot about the unfolded clothes. In reality, I might decide to eat a snack while I watched a show instead of folding clothes. In reality, the pile of unfolded laundry on my bed surprised and annoyed me at bedtime, and I moved the pile onto the nearby dresser. I was too tired to fold laundry.

The day I started folding laundry as I took it out of the dryer, my house looked shockingly better. Laundry disappeared. Honestly, at first it was freaky not seeing piles of clean clothes in random places. I was especially surprised that folding and putting clean clothes away immediately didn't make laundry day take longer. Actually, it went faster. Laundry was completely done in one day, without mountains of clean clothes waiting to be folded.

In case you're wondering, I don't have a folding table. I stack folded clothes on top of the dryer and washing machine. When a stack starts teetering, I put it away. It takes less than ten minutes to fold clothes (and/or hang them on hangers) and put them away. Don't believe me? Time yourself.

USE VINEGAR TO CURE STINKY LAUNDRY

L aundry routines have made this super-useful tip almost obsolete in my house. Almost, but not obsolete enough to not be sure I always have white vinegar in the house.

If you've ever left a load of laundry in the washing machine for too long (especially in the summer), you likely have smelled that funky smell. It's even worse when you smell it while you're wearing something that went all the way through the dryer and into your closet.

I have a rule that if I smell even the slightest whiff of a wonky odor, I rewash.

Before I rewash, I pour white vinegar generously (*generously* means I don't measure) over the top of the wet clothing that is going to be rewashed, smack-dab on top of the clothes. The vinegar won't hurt anything. Add detergent again and rewash the load. If it's an option, use the extra-rinse feature on your washing machine. If you don't have that feature, do a smell test when the load is done, and then run a rinse-only cycle if needed.

CONSIDER MATH IN YOUR LAUNDRY

I'm a fan of laundry detergent pods. I didn't try them for a long time because I'm cheap, and I didn't think they would make much of a difference, but when I tried them once, I was hooked. The ease of grabbing a pod and avoiding the mess of powder or liquid detergent makes me irrationally giddy.

But honestly, it never occurred to me to put more than one pod in a load. Depending on the size of your load of clothes, or the dirtiness of your load of clothes, you likely need to use two pods or even three.

If you're anti-pod, that's fine. Just know that you also need to adjust the amount of laundry detergent you use according to your load size and dirtiness too.

When I didn't have a laundry routine, I was always behind on laundry, so I always had more than I could get done in one session.

When I did do laundry, I wanted the effort to count. I packed as many dirty clothes as I possibly could into my washing machine.

I now realize how much extra stress I was causing myself by doing it the wrong way. Clothes don't get as clean when they don't have any room to move around in the washing machine.

Fill the machine, but don't smush them so you can fit more.

Likewise, clothes dry better when they aren't packed full in the dryer. I'm embarrassed to write this "tip" since it feels so obvious, but I had to learn the hard way that my attempts to get the "most out of my efforts" was backfiring.

An extra benefit my Uncle Eddie pointed out was that when you have fewer clothes in the dryer, they come out less wrinkled. With less room to tumble, clothes stay bunched up.

Realizing I wasn't actually getting my clothes as clean or wrinkle-free as possible because of my desire to get more done with less effort motivated me to change how I did things.

Part 10

SENTIMENTAL CLUTTER

KEEP ONE AND USE IT UP

We talked about Keepsake Boxes and bringing loved ones' things into your home in the section about applying the Container Concept, but let's talk a little more about sentimental clutter. These are the things, or categories of things, that bring up so many memories that our hearts hurt over the thought of letting them go.

When I realize it is time to declutter a category of things that represent a phase of life that is over, I tell myself that I

can keep one. I'm acknowledging it's okay to feel feelings over these baby clothes or toddler toys or my mother-in-law's pots and pans.

But I can't keep everything.

I keep one favorite baby outfit from each of my kids on the shelf in my master bedroom closet. I know where they are, and I run across them every once in a while and my mama heart aches a little. But that's a good feeling. And it's a *much* better feeling than the frustration I used to feel when I stubbed my toe on a box full of baby clothes in my garage. A box full of baby clothes makes life harder and ends up being something I resent. A cute little baby outfit is something I cherish.

Keep one.

USE IT UP

One of my best strategies for letting go of sentimental stuff is to use it. Sometimes, this means I use it up. If I use a burp cloth to wipe bathroom cabinets, I see the burp cloth more often than if I kept it in a box in the attic. I appreciate it more because it's part of my everyday life.

But usually, I use it up. By using something, whether a burp cloth or a coffee cup or blanket, it eventually wears out, and by the time that happens, I'm willing to let go because it has served a purpose.

DECLUTTER PHOTOS

Photos feel important. But just like every other decluttering scenario, the Container Concept applies. Determine the space you have available to devote to photos in your home, and then use that as your limit.

Don't freak out. Start by giving yourself permission to look through the photos and get rid of the trash—the doubles, or pictures of shoes, or school photos of people you never met.

Once you've done that, fill the container you have for photos with your favorites first. I know it's hard, but let that be the limit. It's fine to get another container, but be realistic about what else in your home will have to go to make room for another photo container.

CREATE SHARABLE HEIRLOOMS WITH OLD FAMILY PHOTOS

I have made a few family photo albums by digitizing old family photos. The beauty of doing this (rather large) project is that you can print multiple copies of the same album, so you can give copies to other family members. It's a great way

to create a special Christmas gift and take care of everyone on your list for that side of the family!

Instead of scanning photos, I find it much simpler and quicker to take pictures of the photos with my digital camera or my phone. It works best to put the old photos on a wall with tape or Sticky Tack to take the pictures. If you lay them down and stand over them, it is more difficult to get a photo (of the photo) without a shadow falling on it.

DON'T START WITH THE HARD STUFF

My best advice for decluttering sentimental stuff is to not start with it. If thinking about decluttering a certain category of stuff takes your breath away, don't start with that stuff! Start by decluttering easy stuff. Get rid of things you don't care about. Doing this will do one of two things.

You'll gain decluttering experience and you'll learn how nice it is to live in a house with less stuff. Because of this experience you'll gain, when you get to the difficult stuff, it will look different to you and you may be able to let some of it go more easily.

Or, you may clear out enough space in your home that you'll have room to keep the stuff you love and give it the safe place of honor that it deserves.

FINAL THOUGHTS

Whether you flipped through this book or read every word, I hope you feel more relaxed now than you did when you picked it up. I hope you feel that way because you experienced many "Oh, I could totally do that" moments.

The biggest change I've made in my home has been my commitment to live in it. Right now. My goal for each strategy in this book is to make it easier for you to live in your home. I want you to have clean clothes to wear every day and a kitchen you can cook in without having to dig out a place to work, whether you are making beef bourguignon or grilled cheese sandwiches. I want you to be able to relax in the evening, watching a show or enjoying a hobby, without nagging guilty feelings about all the things you should be doing instead of resting.

The path from a cluttered and messy home to one that isn't a disaster is difficult to find, and it can feel impossible to follow. My goal is to show you the path and to share the hope that it is possible to change your home. The process will take lots of work and give you some sore muscles, but it can be done.

As I decluttered, I realized how much of my home I hadn't been able to truly live in before. I have added a large room's worth of square footage to our home by decluttering. Our livable space is significantly larger than it was before. It's the same home but with more space. I never would have imagined that was possible until I experienced it.

As I started doing small tasks consistently, my house went from crazy to not crazy, and it stayed not crazy as I kept doing the tasks. I was so surprised at how much less time I felt like I was spending working on my house. I was finally doing the things that mattered, and doing those things every day made doing them so much easier.

Most of all, I had no idea the impact the state of my home had on my brain's ability to relax. When I looked at my house as a whole, saw it was messy, and thought the only way to solve the problem was to change everything about it and everything about me, I felt constant nagging feelings. I felt I shouldn't be relaxing because of all the things I thought I should be doing.

Knowing what to do and doing those things (even most of the time) has changed that. I know to do the dishes. When I'm overwhelmed or when I'm on fire, that's where I start.

I know to do a five-minute pickup when the house is starting to feel out of control. I know that when a five-minute pickup doesn't cut it, I need to declutter.

Knowing what to do matters almost as much as doing it.

(Almost.) Knowing what to do makes me like my home, and liking my home helps me enjoy my life.

I hope you accept my gift of sharing what I learned as I stumbled through, so you can get there faster, and hopefully with less angst. Now, go do the dishes.

ABOUT THE AUTHOR

Dana K. White is a blogger, podcaster, speaker, and (much to her own surprise) a decluttering expert. In an attempt to get her home under control, Dana started blogging as "Nony" (short for anonymous) at *A Slob Comes Clean*. Dana soon realized she was not alone in her housekeeping struggles and in her feelings of shame. Today, Dana shares realistic home management strategies with her signature humor and a message of hope for the hopelessly messy through her blog, weekly podcasts, and videos. Dana lives with her husband and three kids just outside of Dallas, Texas.